Praise for
She's Had a Baby—and I'm Having a M[illegible]*wn*

"Let's 'play ball' with fatherhood!"

—ERNIE BANKS, Hall of Fame [illegible]

"James Barron manages to be both light[illegible] [illegible] he leads fellow dads through the pitfalls of babyhoo[illegible] [illegible]ant, he helps a new parent hang on to the sheer joy of these m[illegible] years."

—SYLVIA ANN HEWLETT, president, National Parenting Association

"James Barron has hit a second home run with his sequel *She's Had a Baby.* A serious guide to fathering, served with humor and charm that both parents will find extremely useful."

—CLARICE J. KESTENBAUM, M.D., professor of clinical psychiatry, College of Physicians and Surgeons, Columbia University

"This book can help a couple adjust to the vast changes that parenthood brings about, handle the new stresses, and strengthen their marriage in the process."

—LINDA CARTER, Ph.D., director, Family Studies Program, New York University Child Study Center

"*She's Had a Baby* is a humorous book that walks new parents through the intricate maze of fatherhood with survival techniques and wisdom."

—DR. JANE GREER, family and marriage therapist and author of *How Could You Do This to Me?: Learning to Trust After Betrayal*

Praise for
She's Having a Baby—and I'm Having a Breakdown

"Finally, a book for the father-to-be that treats him like he had something to do with the pregnancy."

—Michael J. Fox

"A lighthearted but practical guide for the rattled fifth wheel at Baby's birth: Daddy."

—Tom Wolfe

"The author handles a wealth of material with more than a little laugh-out-loud wisdom."

—*Child* (chosen as a Best Parenting Book of 1998)

"Mr. Barron has written a sensitive, humorous, and useful book for expectant fathers. I will recommend it to our clients. In fact, I already have. Good work!"

—Elena de Karplus, director, Tokyo Childbirth Education Association

BY THE AUTHOR OF

She's Having a Baby—
and I'm Having a Breakdown

She's Had a Baby

—AND I'M HAVING A MELTDOWN

APPLES

She's Had a Baby

—AND I'M HAVING A MELTDOWN

What Every New Father Needs to Know About Marriage, Sex, and Diapers

James Douglas Barron

QUILL
WILLIAM MORROW
NEW YORK

It is the policy of William Morrow and Company, Inc., and its imprints and affiliates, recognizing the importance of preserving what has been written, to print the books we publish on acid-free paper, and we exert our best efforts to that end.

Library of Congress Cataloging-in-Publication Data
Barron, James Douglas.
She's had a baby—and I'm having a meltdown : what every new father needs to know about marriage, sex, and diapers / James Douglas Barron.
p. cm.
ISBN 0-688-16823-X
1. Fathers—United States—Psychology. 2. Fathers—United States—Attitudes. 3. Father and child—United States. 4. Husbands—United States—Psychology. I. Title.
HQ756.B38 1999 99-11070
306.874'2—dc21 CIP

Printed in the United States of America

First Edition

6 7 8 9 10

BOOK DESIGN BY ANN GOLD

www.williammorrow.com

For Jeannette, Isabelle, and Benjamin

CONTENTS

INTRODUCTION

I was carrying our five-day-old infant over our apartment's threshold when I glanced back at my wife. This was a scene I had envisioned for weeks: I would carry our baby through first and set her down in her bassinet; she'd ogle me, coo, and fall into a wonderful slumber; my wife would throw her arms around my neck; I'd gallantly swoop her off her feet (no strain, no huffing); then, I'd pause at the threshold, kiss her (one of those showy kisses from a 1940s movie) and mutter deeply, "Welcome home." Her eyes would be glimmering. . .

Well, it wasn't quite like that.

Still weak from her C-section, my wife smiled back feebly at my attempt at romance and mumbled something about a rain check. Although she had been navigating the hospital corridors energetically, she was now leaning on our banister railing, out of breath and wobbly.

After I helped my wife walk into the apartment, we stumbled around—strangers in a strange land. Finally, my wife plopped down on the living room couch. There was a millisecond of quiet.

Then, everything happened at once. Our baby wailed piteously, my wife's breasts became clogged, and while I searched for the Extra Strength Tylenol, our phone began ringing off the hook with well-wishers and family. I listened to a dozen well-meaning but long-winded messages on our answering machine and one short one informing us that our baby nurse was a no-show. I tried to calm our baby, called my wife's doctor, whipped up some lunch, and fell onto the couch beside my wife. Then, I started to laugh.

Like every man in my shoes, I pondered The Future, but became immediately aware that here it was, slamming through the walls of our living room like some runaway train. My eyes took in my desk, piled high with work and bills. Suddenly, I blurted out, "How are we going to do all this? The most I've ever cared for is a golden retriever!"

"We'll be okay," my wife answered. I fixed her a cup of coffee while she began reading one of her books about the baby's first year.

Later (at her insistence), I peeked at her book. I was hoping for some guidance on early fatherhood but was instantly turned off by the book's technical tone. I was overwhelmed by its detail, and the damned thing was nearly seven hundred pages. My reaction was that of millions of men before me: *I don't know any guy who could read this!* Like those men, I didn't like reading a book written for women. I felt like a trespasser. I wondered why so little attention was paid to the change in the marriage after the baby is born—when every new father senses he needs guidance there, too. I needed a commonsense guide written for guys like me, who often go to the sports pages before anything else in the newspaper. I wanted a book that would teach me how to enjoy fatherhood, how to keep my marriage vital, how to help my wife adjust, how to juggle work and home responsibilities, and how to keep the zip in our sex life. That's when I knew I had to write a book to help men (and the women married to new dads) through this wonderful insanity.

I wanted to write a book so new fathers can rip into fatherhood—and know it can be a blast. Lots of new fathers sense a change in the air and want to get away from the stodgy image of father from the past . . . but they don't know how to get there. That's what this book is about: Realizing fatherhood is a beginning, not an end. Yeah, the early months of fatherhood *are* zany. Hopefully, this book will help new dads feel less alone in their feelings and less like they're bushwhacking through the thicket of fatherhood with only a toothpick in hand.

Take your new future one day at a time. . .

—JAMES DOUGLAS BARRON

P.S. I realize that a lot of couples with babies aren't married, but for simplicity's sake, throughout the book I've referred to the baby's mother as "wife."

THE 10 GREATEST MOMENTS OF EARLY FATHERHOOD:

1. Snuggling with your wife and baby in bed.
2. Walking into the baby's room and seeing your baby's first smile.
3. Waking up in the morning, feeling refreshed, and realizing you actually slept through the night.
4. Finally understanding what your own parents went through.
5. Watching your baby crawl across the floor, sit up, and clap.
6. Hearing your baby say, "Da-da."
7. Cheering as your baby teeters across the room on two feet and falls into your arms.
8. Feeling lightheaded when your baby kisses you for the first time.
9. Taking your toddler to the ballpark wearing identical ball caps and eating hot dogs together.
10. Having amazing sex with your wife (and realizing sex isn't an old suitcase you left at the station back there, "Before Baby").

1. SURVIVAL DAYS: The First Month

1. She's had the baby! Bravo!

It's great; it's wonderful . . . So why are you staring at the ceiling at four A.M.? Because, like all guys, you're afraid of the Unknown (and you've noticed that babies don't come with operating manuals.)

So stop holding your breath, exhale, and take a cue from your wife. Right now, your marching orders are to take it one day at a time.

2. If being a father is so natural, how come you're doing things like eating a pastrami sandwich at 6:45 A.M.?

Life before fatherhood had its basic stops and starts—known to normal people as day and night, and breakfast, lunch, and dinner. But soon after our baby was born, my wife caught me scarfing down a pastrami sandwich before seven A.M. "That's revolting!" she said.

I halted in mid-bite. I should have been disgusted, but I wasn't. Time, as I'd known it, no longer existed. I'd been up pretty much for four days straight. I'd adjusted to catnapping at three P.M. (which I now considered my night's sleep), eating cereal for dinner as breakfast, eating a sandwich for lunch at breakfast time, and eating whatever caught my eye (and it was plenty) for dinner at midday. Sleep was a herky-jerky train ride with stops wherever the conductor (and there was little doubt who *that* was: our baby) desired. I barely recognized my wife. She was so pawed, sucked, pinched, and gummed that I knew *never* to touch her. Her lips were still parched from labor. She walked like she'd just taken a mule ride down the Grand Canyon. She was drugged, groggy, achy. Seeking quiet, we dashed into closets to make phone calls, and neither of us thought it odd that we tugged on the telephone cord if we needed the phone. Our parents were driving us nuts with constant, elated phone calls; the pediatrician seemed smiley and expensive but basically unhelpful; and our friends seemed like distant, cool moons that had shifted their orbit from our solar system to somebody else's. All in all, our world was upside down.

Yet despite all that, we were in heaven. It's amazing how adaptable we humans are when we're in love. And this was love. Big-time, uppercut to the jaw, knockout, seeing-stars love. I'd never felt anything like it. The day after we got married, my wife and I were very naughty in a boathouse, not fifteen feet from sun worshipers. We could hear the slap of hamburger patties hitting the grill and the flap of sails of boats pointing into the wind . . . and I thought, *It doesn't get much better than this.*

Ah, but it does. That's the big secret of all this early infant madness: You can now imagine your life without the boathouse love scene, but you can't imagine your life without this crying, defecating, arm-waving, nearly cross-eyed baby. Just take a whiff of your baby's neck. What's that smell? Love.

So, for a while, you'll survive on love (and 6:45 A.M. pastrami sandwiches).

6 THINGS YOU'LL REALIZE THE FIRST WEEK AFTER BRINGING YOUR BABY HOME:

1. Pregnancy was *nothing* compared to this!
2. The change from Single Man to Married Man is *nothing* compared to the change from Married Man to Father.
3. You never thought you'd think this, but you want your mother-in-law (or the blue-haired nanny) to stay *forever.*
4. You can't take the baby out without bringing more stuff than an Everest climbing team (and IMAX film crew).
5. You really are truly exhausted, because when you peed while holding your glasses in your mouth, you also yawned—and had to fish them out of the toilet bowl.
6. You can change a diaper while talking to your mother no one line and your mother-in-law on the other, while winking to your wife that you've got it all under control.

3. There will be a series of reminders that your baby is real.

One moment might be when you see your baby's name written and suddenly, she will seem *very* real. When we started getting gifts in the mail (especially checks made out to our newborn), I thought, "You know, this isn't for me. It's not for my wife. There truly is a baby here." (Yes, it sounds weird, but this will happen to you, too.)

4. Turn off the ringer on the phone and the speaker on the answering machine.

Play back messages in the late afternoon and return calls all at one time. Otherwise, you'll both go crazy from the well-intentioned but incessant calls from curious and concerned family members and friends.

ONE OF THE MOST IMPORTANT THINGS YOU CAN DO FOR YOUR CHILD IS REMAIN HAPPILY MARRIED. Yes, getting involved as a father is fabulous—but not to the exclusion of focusing on your wife. Wear different hats: father, husband, lover, friend, confidant.

---

5. Trust your instincts.

My buddy Tim said, "I had never held a baby before in my life, and there I was, an hour after driving back from the hospital, our baby at my hip while I was cooking breakfast for my wife." The answers aren't really in the baby development books; they're in you.

6. If you don't trust your instincts, know that it's not* that *hard to hold your baby.

How is it you could catch a muddy pigskin thrown by a quarterback with a dislocated shoulder on a day that made a monsoon look like a sun shower—and you can't hold a baby? The answer: You're afraid your baby's head will fall off and roll down the street like some lopsided cantaloupe . . . all because you're a clumsy oaf.

Don't get me wrong; you have to be extremely careful with your baby's neck. So, here's how: The football hold is good. Your baby lies across your forearm; your hand holds your baby's head; your wrist supports your baby's weak neck. Or your baby's head over your left shoulder, left arm to your baby's fanny, right hand supporting your baby's back. Or cradle your baby in the nook of your arm, his head near your armpit, his feet near your wrists. Or the two-armed baby to your chest hold. Or the two-armed rocking baby motion.

It's hard to go wrong because, well, holding a baby is natural. One day, I came across a diorama of cave dwellers in a museum of natural history and I had the eeriest sensation. The hairy dude in the diorama was holding his baby daughter in almost the same position I was holding my baby daughter.

---

9 THINGS A NEW FATHER FEARS MOST ABOUT FATHERHOOD:

1. No matter how hard I'll try to protect our baby, something will go wrong.

2. My wife loves our baby more than me.
3. Sex as I've known it is over.
4. Leisure time as I've known it is over.
5. Adventure as I've known it is over.
6. My youth as I've known it is over.
7. My wife will always be demanding, irritable, inconsolable, crazy, achy, tired, bad-mannered, and addicted to Extra Strength Tylenol.
8. I'll become a lethally dull, gin-and-tonic-guzzling, work-complaining, short-fused, business-page-reading, pot-bellied paradigm of fatherhood.
9. I'll become divorced from my wife, fall for a bleached-blond second wife, wear a silver toupee and a navy blazer and gray slacks and loafers with gold bridle chains, see my kid on Wednesdays and every other weekend, and work at a job I hate—to pay the college tuition of a son who sides with his mother.

---

7. Don't ever say you'd wished for a boy baby if you get a girl.

Okay, maybe in the back of your skull, you'd always wished for a boy, so you could climb the Rockies or shoot bottles off a fence or play soldiers or have someone to see sci-fi movies with. But girls do all that, too. Or maybe you always related to girls better and heard from your buddies that there's no greater love than that of a Little Girl for her Daddy.

Well, get with it! Break all the gender stereotypes, thank the heavens for your healthy baby, and enjoy what you've got.

8. Try not to inspect your wife's episiotomy stitches.

A few days after our second baby's birth, my wife asked if I'd take a peek. "It hurts so much and I just want to be sure it's okay," she explained. Gulp. Hmmm . . . I had checked out her C-section stitches from our first delivery without any qualms. But that was an abdomen and this was, well, a part of her anatomy that meant a lot to me.

Big mistake. I felt as if I were under the hood of a car knowing nothing about engines. How did I know if healing was proceeding as it should?

I stood up, hugged my wife closely, and whispered, "You look great. No problem." Then I added casually, "Your doctor should do all further inspections. She's the real expert." Sure, you'll get over it if you look, but if you're like me, you just don't need this in your memory bank.

9. Help your wife deal with her feelings about the birth.

Maybe your wife had a three-hour labor, squeezed out the baby, didn't listen to doctor's orders, and right after was doing jumping jacks and wind sprints down the hospital corridor. But probably not. It's up to you to help her confront what she may view as her "delivery shortcomings." Maybe she had an obstetrician (like our first one) who called her a wimp and threw down his rubber gloves and stomped out the door during labor. She might have pleaded for more painkilling drugs during delivery when all along she'd hoped to get along without them. She might *feel* she wasn't as good at delivery as she'd hoped (or as her mother always claimed to be with her four children's births).

When I asked my wife, she said, "I can't remember huge blocks of time. It's a blur." If your wife says the same thing, don't say, "Honey, it's called drugs." Rather, tell her that delivery amnesia is one of God's gifts to women (it allows them to have another child). Or blame it on sensory overload. Here's a chance for you to show your concern and care—two qualities that are especially useful while your wife recovers.

10. Keep alert for postpartum depression.

Every new parent feels overwhelmed—at least partly. But sinking into a clinical depression after childbirth, which happens to some new mothers or fathers, is something else. If your mood or hers is constantly down, get help.

YOUR WIFE'S GREATEST FEARS OF MOTHERHOOD:

1. Something will go wrong with the baby, no matter how good a mother she is.
2. You'll leave her for a twenty-seven-year-old blonde who can eat *anything* and still wear spandex shorts without a sweatshirt tied around her waist.

3. She'll always think of sex as that thing she used to enjoy doing and now does with the dutiful diligence of Mother Teresa calming the ill.
4. She'll never get rid of her belly pouch (and she'll always be grabbing it when nobody's looking and trying to wish it away).
5. She'll never have a career again—or, if she does, she'll be so shrouded in guilt (over not being a good enough mother) that she'll hate every minute of it.
6. The baby will love you more because you entertain while she nags and cooks and cleans and folds the laundry and takes him for shots.
7. Gray hair.
8. Her hands are an indication that an *Invasion of the Body Snatchers*–type transformation is taking place: she's becoming her mother!

---

11. Are you secretly wondering if delivering a baby was a sexual experience for your wife?

Some of my buddies confessed they were, shall we say, *curious.* I asked a bunch of my female friends, and the response varied from, "Uch! Are you kidding?!" to "I thought I was going to puke!" to "About as sexy as root canal work" to "If sex is about fulfilling my role as a woman, then yeah, the delivery was sexy."

If you really need to know, go ahead and ask.

12. Keep quiet about Male Weirdness.

We know it's true: Men can be really bizarre. Every dad checks out his infant son's organ pretty carefully. (It starts early. One buddy said he pointed to the sonogram screen and blurted, "Hung like a horse!" One of the lab techs turned to my friend's wife and said, "They all think that.") Another new father admitted that when he saw his one-day-old son's penis, he threw his arms up in the air and yelled, "Yes!" (His baby's penis was only reacting to hormones in the birth canal and assumed normal proportions the next day.)

Why this fixation? Simple: We all want the little guy to start life with every advantage. None of this will make any sense to your wife. Best not to share it. Instead, say something about your infant's angelic lips or long lashes (the envy of all womankind) or his rounded buns (another envy of womankind) or his little clenched fists with the perfect fingernails or the way he clutches on to your neck when you hold him . . . or a million other fine things.

13. Relax about your baby's imperfections.

The journey through the birth canal can take a toll on your baby's appearance. (C-section babies usually took less misshapen and less pocked by forceps impressions.) No, you didn't get the brand of baby they show you in the movies: perfectly coifed locks, not a pimple in sight, round head, and look-straight-in-the-camera eye contact. You got what everybody else got: a cone head with slightly crossed eyes, a facial rash (that reminds you of your teenage face after a night of French fries, pizza, and chocolate), squished features, and a soft spot on top of his head that's really scary because it throbs and jiggles.

Your wife or your baby's pediatrician will remind you that your baby is still looking beat up from the birth process.

14. Find a favorite song for your baby and play it often.

It doesn't have to be some sappy song by Raffi. I chose a song by John Lee Hooker and Carlos Santana called "The Healer" and my wife would crack up watching me boogie around our living room with our weeks-old baby, twirling, dipping, hamming it up.

Now when I play the song, I say to my daughter, "We danced to that one hundreds of times." She'll reply, "Oh, yeah, I remember!" Everyone who hears this chuckles (who could have such a memory?), but I've got an impossible-to-prove theory that it all sinks in somewhere. Anyway, the memory makes me feel damned good.

15. Your wife may not find breast-feeding easy (at first).

Nobody warns you how hard it's going to be. Here's what my female friends said: "I woke up two days after giving birth and my breasts were so heavy, I thought the ceiling plaster had fallen down on my chest during the night!" And: "I dug my toes into the carpet it hurt so much." And: "While I nursed, I watched cobwebs grow." And: "Breast-feeding is for the birds."

And: "I had so much milk, I literally begged my husband to please relieve me. He wouldn't! I got mad and threatened to put it in his coffee! Finally, I said, 'Both of us are crazy!' "

My wife had some initial problems with clogging, and I had absolutely no idea what to do. I called her obstetrician and tried the hot packs she recommended. Soon we solved the problem. Within a few days, she looked at me while she was nursing and said, "Isn't this a trip? If you told me ten years ago I'd be doing this, I'd never have believed you!"

Your response is important. Tell her if you find it beautiful (contrary to popular rumor, some men aren't challenged by the baby's monopoly over their wives' breasts). If you feel uncomfortable with your wife's nursing, try to understand why (so you can get over it). It's your job to keep your wife from giving up too easily during the early, tough stage. Breast milk is free and convenient, has great health benefits for your baby (fewer colds and ear infections), and tastes natural to your baby. Breast-feeding is old-fashioned, creates a strong bond between mother and baby, and might help your wife lose her pregnancy weight.

16. Relax about breast-feeding in public—and about other guys who like to get a peek.

Okay, you hate it when some dude is talking to your wife (and getting a good eyeful) while she's nursing the baby. Your first impulse is to slug him. But admit it: A young woman nursing a child is an attractive thing to see, and you've always been curious, too, in similar situations.

Most guys don't mean to look; they can't help it. Really, who knows where to look when your wife whips out her breast for the baby when you're with friends—or even in public? Besides, attitudes toward breast-feeding have changed. Women nurse their babies in restaurants, parks, airports.

So don't make a fool of yourself by shielding her. Or telling her to go to another room (or rest room). Or shooting menacing stares at potential peepers. Instead, get your signals straight with your wife: Maybe she tilts her head and clears her throat when she wants you to tell a creep to get lost. Otherwise, it's her body and she has her own well-developed sense of privacy.

17. Her breasts have new meaning.

As soon as my wife began breast-feeding, I could nearly make out an invisible sign over her chest that read PROPERTY OF BABY, and that was okay as far as she was concerned. And her breasts were initially locked up in a heavy-duty nursing bra that had all the allure of two jockstraps stitched together.

"I just can't wear these," my wife said, tossing her nursing bras into a drawer. "Come with me," I said, "we're going bra shopping." If you really want to feel like a hero, bring your wife and baby to a lingerie shop and listen to the saleswoman rave about your consideration. It's money well spent: It means your wife can feel sexy.

Don't forget to take a photo of your wife breast-feeding. This gesture, too, goes a long way toward showing you're not feeling left out.

18. Buy a breast pump for your wife.

The baby store talked us into renting a mega-pump with all sorts of fancy features like the double-suction unit that would allow her to express milk from both boobs at once. But when my wife tried it out behind a closed door it sounded as if she were jackhammering through the plaster wall. "You okay in there?" I yelled. "The hell with this thing!" she said, opening the door. "It's strong enough for liposuction." We returned it and settled on a little orange handheld electric model, which also ran on batteries—a handy option.

No woman loves a breast pump. "I feel like a cow," my wife said on numerous occasions. "And don't ask to watch." (I didn't argue that one . . .) If you do watch, don't make jokes—even though it's incredibly funny-looking. Your wife has got to relieve herself of milk periodically or just the thought of your baby might be enough to soil her favorite shirt. Help her find one she can take with her, so she can express milk at inconvenient times and places, such as parties where the bathroom is otherwise occupied, forcing her to sit atop a pile of jackets on the bed.

19. Learn how to bottle-feed your baby.

Here's the cliché: Thanks to your wife's magic milk machines, you feel neglected, sulk in the corner, and wait for the world to pity you.

Thankfully, you can participate—by using either milk she pumped into bottles or formula in bottles. And it's not all that hard. Keep the bottle so the nipple stays full (any air in the bottle will become gas in your baby's tummy). Talk calmly, soothingly. Enjoy the urgency of the baby's feeding. Then, pay special attention to that delicious moment when your infant falls into deep slumber and you feel the weight of her body slip into your arms.

20. Become a burping wizard.

If you don't burp your baby every five or ten minutes, he'll feel full, when it's only air that's expanding his tummy. When he gets that pained expression, don't panic and hand your baby over to your wife. You can try holding your baby up to your shoulder and rubbing in a gentle, circular motion on his back. Or you may prefer having your baby sit up on your thigh while you support his front with one hand while the other rubs his back. (Pay special attention to supporting his head and neck in this position.) Or try laying your baby over your lap and rub one or both hands on his back to coax a burp. Say encouraging things to your baby while you coax a burp.

Don't pretend your baby's back is a bongo drum or you'll get a stare from your wife that could boil water. And be sure to keep a cloth over your shoulder or you'll have a closet filled with splotched shirts.

IF YOUR BABY CANNOT STOP CRYING, TRY ONE MORE BURP.

---

21. Keep two dozen bottle nipples on hand at all times.

Those damned things go bad sooner than you'd think, and at this stage in new parenthood the smallest baby-related problem can escalate into a full-blown crisis. (Forgetting to buy the right brand of formula becomes major!) In our house, shot nipples turned into *Red Alert! Everyone to their battle stations! Now, whose turn was it to buy nipples? Fire accusations . . . !*

Just make it your job. Be resourceful and buy two dozen of them. (The cost is nothing compared to an hour of marital counseling.)

22. Go ahead, show off your baby!

Bring your baby to your bakery or to your coffee shop or to a museum or to a park—just so you can watch people's reactions. Total strangers will exclaim, "Oh, how adorable!" and offer their seats on buses and on park benches. You'll feel the *threeness* of your new family. All this goes a long way toward putting your fatigue on the back burner.

23. But be prepared for irritating behavior from visitors.

Everybody's curious to see you as parents, but you sometimes wonder if they think you're *really* parents or you're only *acting* like it—which ticks you off, because by the first week, you've earned your stripes and you *feel* like a parent.

Then there's the "Who the Baby Looks Like" game—also irritating, mainly because it's an insipid game (the baby's looks change every few weeks), but also because the assumption is that the baby couldn't possibly look like a mix of both of you—that would be too easy, too kind. One "friend" told me, "I'm so relieved she looks like your wife. Your looks wouldn't translate into a girl. Girls who look like their dads are really cursed," and so on. It was times like this I wanted my baby to have a bout of projectile vomiting.

And here's what you say: "Visiting hours are over." It's simple: You're in control, and you don't need it. You don't have time for it.

Otherwise, your baby will get overstimulated, and after everyone leaves, she'll cry for hours. Next time, tell them to leave before that happens.

THINGS YOU DON'T WANT TO HEAR FROM VISITORS BUT WILL ANYWAY:

1. "Boy or a girl? A girl! No. I don't believe it. She looks like a boy! I bet everyone tells you that!"
2. "I bet she's an easy baby."
3. "She's petite. But that's cute in a girl."
4. "Do you have all your toes? We'll have to count . . . ?"
5. "Where's your nose? I've got your nose! It's right here behind your ear! You want it back? Oh, no! Now it's behind your daddy's ear."
6. "Do you like your mother and father? I didn't think so. Why don't you come home with me?"
7. "How much do you weigh? Now, if you were a turkey, I'd say you were rather small."
8. "What's my name? Huh? I know you know it. That's right: *Jer-ald.* Now, what's my last name? Huh? I know you know it . . . "
9. "Do you know how we're related? Well, your daddy's father's uncle's son was married to my grandfather's

half-sister from the second marriage. Know what that makes us?"

10. "What's that you've got up your nose? Is that a big booger? Is it? I think it *is-s-z-z-z . . .* "

---

24. Don't be overly paranoid when other people hold your baby.
I know I was with our first child—and it drove my wife nuts.

We were at a Thanksgiving dinner at my great-aunt's with some baby-adoring distant relatives I'd never met. Society has an unwritten law that anyone without felony charges can hold anyone's baby, so long as they show good intent. I didn't buy it. Maybe Uncle Max has a cold . . . maybe those claws on Aunt Gertrude will accidentally scratch the baby. . . . So they were playing Pass the Baby and I lost it and burst out, "I think that's enough, now!" and took our baby back. Everyone looked mystified.

At the time, I thought I was doing my Daddy Protective Thing; now, I realize I went a bit overboard. By the time we had our second child, I felt freer letting people hold him.

25. You won't believe how much you'll have to think about diapers. 
Whether they're dry or wet or "full" (you'll actually jam your nose up close and sniff!), how often you need to buy them and which types fit best or fasten most securely are now *major* concerns.

26. You cannot escape changing diapers.

Every dad has to change diapers—it's part of the job description of fatherhood today. My friend Lena said, "My husband imagined he could change five diapers per baby. I said, *'Hello-oh-o!¿ We're in this together!'* " Eventually, most dads get over their squeamishness and get pretty good at changing wet diapers (practice makes perfect).

But guys deal with poop differently than women. Don't let it bother you that your wife gets annoyed because you waste huge amounts of baby wipes or use more ointment or have a special way of cleaning around (and behind) your son's balls. You're treating it like a military problem, a mop-up operation that requires maximum firepower, and she's got a daintier approach. Well, you're entitled to your own style.

In diapers, timing is everything. Never change a diaper after your baby has drifted off to dreamland immediately following a good feeding (if you do, your moment of quiet may be shattered by piercing screams). Create a calm mood, get your baby's eye contact, exude confidence from your fingertips. No matter how gruesome the odor, don't holler insults into the air, or cringe, or fan your face.

The last time you were this nervous with your fingertips was when you unsnapped your first bra in high school. Diapers are a whole lot easier than that . . .

27. If you have to, knock yourself out trying other types of diapers, then use disposables.

All sorts of cool movie stars bragged about using washable diapers, so my wife and I decided to give them a whirl. Besides, I've long been, well, an Environmental Fanatic (I go ballistic when a basketball is shipped in a thousand Styrofoam bubbles). So I was going to be damned if my baby would ever see a disposable diaper and undermine my stance.

It was a nice idea, but washables were a total drag. I'm not sure who hated them more: me, my wife, or our baby. They sagged. Our baby wanted a change after the slightest trickle. Our entire apartment smelled like two-day-old Chinese food in a Dumpster. Then we tried environmentally sound disposables, but they were not so great for *our* environment—they dripped and leaked everywhere—and their degradability was in question, too.

I mentioned this to a buddy (and father) over beers one night. He looked straight at me and said, "You're going to use disposable diapers. Why? Because life is too short. If you don't, you'll screw up your marriage, your kid's psyche, your work. Make it up elsewhere. Get solar power. Run your car on apple cider."

We switched immediately. Still, I sometimes grimace when I drive past a landfill off the New Jersey Turnpike and think, "I'm responsible for some of that." But I try to make it up in other ways.

28. Choose your bathroom terminology with great care (because you will, over the next ten years, utter these words more than any others).

My parents used *wee-wee* and *moo-moo,* which always struck me as more than slightly inane. My wife and I chose the utterly prosaic *peeps* and *poops*—which, of course, my kids will find totally insipid once they're old enough to make that judgment.

29. And remember that poop doesn't just stay in the diaper.

That's right—there will be times when an evil little marble of a turd will escape from the opened diaper and roll behind the radiator, and you will have to get down on your hands and knees with a flashlight and an unbent clothes hanger to retrieve it. Even worse, there will be those lovely times when you pick up the baby and the pressure of your hand under his diapered behind squirts a load of semi-liquid poop up his back, or it runs down into the Michelin-man crevices of his leg. Or when the diaper falls off and you find your baby looking as if she's pretending she's in the mud during Woodstock's rainstorm. So, diaper changing is more of an adventure than you'd expected . . . but you'll adapt.

30. You'll end up knowing the colors of the poop rainbow.

There's a grungy greenish-black turd that your baby will lay into her diaper about a day after birth. It looks like gunk you'd expect to find in a car engine at the 120,000-mile checkup, but it's perfectly normal. Of course, they've got a scary name for it—*meconium*—but all you have to know is it's your infant's way of clearing out the last residue from Life in the Womb.

Then there's the early breast-feeding phase where your baby's poop smells, well, almost okay and looks like curried cottage cheese. You may be tempted to think, "Our baby is so perfect, even her crap smells sweet." Ah, but sooner than you think, you get a real stinker that will send you reeling. And you'll probably discover that your baby's poop during the breast-feeding period can, at times, fly almost across the room (that is, unless you block it). One new father said, "The nurse warned me that this could happen, but I didn't believe her. As soon as I released a diaper (which was only wet), our baby released a yellowish poop that would have gone seven or eight feet if I hadn't been standing in front of it, where it splattered all over me. I considered it a christening of sorts."

After your baby stops breast-feeding, the fumes emanating from the diaper will become incomparably more difficult to take. You'll think, *How could this tender creature create so foul a smell?*

Don't get into the describe-the-stool game with your wife. It's another example of unromantic parental pastimes to avoid.

GET A GOOD WASHER/DRYER. After having a baby, your wife would probably rather have a new washer/dryer than a diamond ring. You'll have ten times more laundry to do than before, and she'll want it ten times cleaner.

---

31. Don't let your wife say, "Never mind. I'll do it myself," as she grabs your baby away from you.

My friend Marina told me her typical conversation with her husband, Caleb, when he was taking care of their baby. She (nervous): "What do you think you're doing?" He (Frank Sinatra tone): "I'm doing it my way." She (anxious): "Well, your way is way too slow." He (defensive): "My way seems all right for me and the baby." She (livid): "Never mind. Just hand her to me. I'll do it myself." Baby (red-faced): *Waaaaah!*

Just do it your way.

32. *Try not to say to your wife, "Here! It's your turn!"*

Let's say your agreed-upon shift ends at midnight, you worked until five-thirty, the baby drove you nuts since six, and it's 11:59 P.M. You watch the diode light switch, tap your wife awake, and say, "She's *all* yours!" Not a good idea. Your communication has already disintegrated into a series of back-and-forth commands—as if you're barking at each other.

I'm not saying you should turn yourself into a wimp, but you and your wife will have to define a new, gentler language in dealing with one another if you want your marriage to come through early parenthood unscathed. Some common courtesies go a long way. And if you say something the wrong way, say, "Oops. What I meant to say was . . . " Then, start over.

33. *If you've had a second or third baby, expect a mix of emotions from an older sibling.*

Our daughter would contradict herself every few minutes. "Hi, Mommy, how's the baby going?" The next minute: "Do you like the baby? More than me?" Then: "He smells like a baby. His hair is so soft." Followed by: "I'm going to chop off his head and throw it into the garbage." Then, trouble sleeping. "I want the night to go away! Pull the night away! I'm going to spank the moon!"

Then: sleeplessness. Right after we brought the new baby home, our daughter stayed up until one A.M. The next day, she climbed into her long-abandoned crib, curled up with her dolls, and pretended to be a baby. But five days later, after arguing that the new baby couldn't use her old crib because it was hers, she said, "Daddy, let's put him in the crib." When we brought him there, she said, "He needs my toy." She lobbed one in. "He needs my doll!"

Lobbed that in, too. Elated, she cried to her brother, "You little lamb chop!"

Could it be over? Only five days of sibling rivalry? Hardly. A few days later, our daughter yelled, "My doll is mad! She wants to smack the baby! She wants him to go back inside Mommy's tummy!"

It's normal for the older sibling to say those things. Don't overreact. Help the older sibling know that she can't act on her thoughts, though. Sure, you're going to end up part policeman, part shrink, part referee, and only partly sane. But who said this would be easy?

GET IN TOUCH WITH THE NOW-I-KNOW-WHY-I'M-ON-THIS-PLANET SENSATION. Don't let the hurricane of responsibilities obscure the vastness of early fatherhood. Doesn't everything that came before seem, well . . . trivial?

---

34. Listen to your baby's heartbeat.

Your wife will find it endlessly endearing that you press your ear to your newborn's tiny chest to listen to the quiet thumping . . . and you'll feel connected to those times you listened to her heartbeat through the stethoscope.

35. Take photos and videos.

No dull posing. The nicely dressed, perfectly primped photos will be *bor-ing* later on. Catch the in-between moments: your wife and baby when she's holding her up in a doorway; when she's kissing your baby's neck; reading. Use soft side lighting (flash and the baby's pupils don't mix). Don't miss a classic photo: your baby's first bath. (And be sure to take a picture when your baby has shampooed curls rising from his head like a Don King hairstyle.) Be sure to have your wife photograph you with your baby, too. Don't be the invisible dad in those photo albums. (And, no, your empathetic pregnancy weight is not an excuse to run from the camera.)

Don't forget to take videos. Videos capture your baby's reflexes, motions, mumblings, first words, first two-toothed smile, and, much later, first game of speed-putt mini-golf. Two general rules: Start each video by saying the date and maybe what's happened before on that day (you'll never remember later on), and stay away from panning shots, which make everyone dizzy to watch.

36. Keep a baby photo with you at all times.

You'll be at work or on a trip and you need a fix. So you'll look at the photo and your eyes will smart. It feels good. It's that simple. Besides, early on, lots of people will ask about the kid and then say, "Have you got a picture with you?"

GET DUPLICATES WHEN YOU PROCESS YOUR BABY PHOTOS AND SEND THEM IMMEDIATELY TO THE GRANDPARENTS. Bring stamped, addressed envelopes when you pick up your film and drop them in the mailbox on your way home. Don't procrastinate, or you'll get a frantic call from the grandparents! (And they're right: they need frequent, up-to-date pictures to feel included—besides, they need photos to show to their friends.)

---

37. Everyone will act like they know everything and you know nothing (or less than nothing).

It's not only total strangers on the street who offer you unasked-for advice. There are all those well-intentioned friends and relatives who are putting in their two cents, particularly your mother and your mother-in-law, who have become the Ann Landers of grandmothers. *They know everything*. You stupidly thought that grandmotherhood might make them feel, well, archaic, but it turns out they know how to burp, feed, change, bathe, calm, rock, breast-feed, smile at, talk to, coo to, coax, coddle, and cozy the baby. And one of them might already be lecturing you on the importance of making the little fellow eat spinach so he'll grow as strong as Popeye.

During those years that you two went to college, graduated, worked, dated, courted, married, and got ready for parenthood, Mom has been waiting to share all she knows about babies. You're miffed. You're upset. This is *your* chance to make your own mistakes, to end up sending your kid to some expensive-but-effective shrink for your own reasons! So you have the automatic urge to say, "Mom, we don't need your input right now."

Don't. It's sometimes tough to take advice (especially from your mom or your mother-in-law), but don't be so pigheaded you can't hear something useful. One of the secret side benefits of babies is that you finally learn to chill out on your parents.

It's also family-building time. Some day, you'll want to feel you have a part in helping your children with their babies—and you don't want to remember what a blazing fool you were by not letting these grandparents help out now.

38. Help your wife write thank you notes.

One friend threw up his arms and said, "I just wish Miss Manners would say it's okay *not* to write thank yous for baby gifts!" Everyone who's ever had a baby knows the last thing you want to do when the baby is asleep is write yet another thank you note for yet another baby rattle.

But it's really embarrassing when you bump into a friend who says, "Hey, did you get that gift I sent you?" Best to help your wife hammer them out quickly. Sit down together for a couple of hours and get it done all at once.

THE BABY'S BEEN HOME A COUPLE OF WEEKS, YOU'VE CAUGHT UP ON SOME SLEEP, AND ALREADY YOU'RE THINKING ABOUT S . . . E . . . X Too bad! It's way too soon. Your sex life is on *pause*. Hang in there. Repeat a dozen times: My sex life will return to normal, my sex life will return to normal, my sex life will return to normal . . .

---

39. Every new father is worried that Sex As He's Known It is over.

Finito. Kaput. Gone, gone, gone . . .

You wonder if your wife will ever again be the hot, lusty creature who thirsted for more and more and more sex. You wonder if she'll always be so tired that she'll be asleep the instant *before* her head hits the pillow. You wonder if she'll always run into a room, hug the baby, kiss

her on the neck a thousand times, proclaim her love over and over—then cast a glance at you and say, "Can you get me a diaper and some wipes, please?"

Let's put this in plain English: Your sex life has changed—but how could it not? Right now, plain old fatigue is dominating your life. There's a dull swirl in the back of your brain that feels like sand filtering through an hourglass. But you'll both learn to get by on less sleep, and eventually, your baby will learn to sleep through the night. Those lusty thoughts that used to drive you to sexual delirium will be on the back burner. When you see Gwyneth or Winona or Nicole in a movie, you'll think, *She's lovely, but I'd rather have a half-hour of uninterrupted sleep.*

Frankly, even when your sex life gets back on track, you'll probably have a tad less sex than you did before you had the baby, but it can be far more gratifying. Some of my female friends said they had far more interest in sex after having the baby. Many felt that having created life was reflected in the sexual bond with their husband.

You have a lot to do with what *your* future sex life will be like. Focus on communicating with your wife and the rest will follow. A character in a Woody Allen film says, "Once the sex goes, it all goes." I'd modify that: Once the communication goes, the sex goes, and then it all goes.

Have patience. And wait until your wife is ready.

40. *Try a shorter work schedule for the next few weeks.*

Right. Not so easy when your boss gives you a pat on the back and then tells you he needs sixty hours' work from you.

But your wife and baby need you, too. And, much to your surprise, your work might pale beside fatherhood, leading you out of the office earlier than usual.

41. Be on time.

One new mother said, "My husband promised he'd be home at seven and he didn't walk in the door until nine-thirty. By then, I was seething. Tears were streaming down my cheeks as I yelled, 'I looked forward to my damned seven o'clock walk all day and now where am I going to go in this damned neighborhood at nearly ten o'clock?!' I cried all the way down the stairs and for most of the walk."

Let your wife know if you're going to be late. And be sure to accept fault when it's yours. From your wife's perspective, there's nothing worse than failing to admit when you've been inconsiderate toward her (it sends the message, *I don't appreciate all you're doing*).

42. Support your wife's new role.

When you were deciding if this woman, now your wife, was *the one,* you might have rated her skills: a great lover, friend, cook, homemaker. Whatever. Now, it all seems to boil down to something you never thought too much about: She's a great mother. She has terrific patience. She doesn't flip out when the baby spits up on her favorite dress. She can juggle *everything.*

Realize that most of her feminine pride is invested in this new venture: mothering. If she fails, she'll be shattered. She needs you to help build her confidence, so tell her, "Our baby couldn't have a better mother."

43. Don't turn your wife into your mother.

Stop for a second and think about it: Who was the last person who told you to clean up so often? To take out the trash? To empty the dishwasher?

There's one way to help ease the constant chiding about chores: Do more. Make a list of what causes the nagging. You'll be surprised how much repetition there is. Here are some possibilities: You don't make the bed or take out the trash or empty the baby's diaper wastebasket or buy new diapers, baby food, formula, or wipes, or you've promised to fix up the nursery for months and you still haven't done it.

Negotiate the list, and then tack it to the inside of your clothes closet door. While you're getting dressed, remind yourself of which minor items you can do today or on the weekend. Then do them.

44. Don't call your wife "Mom."

As in, "It's your turn to change her diaper, Mom." Or "Can you quiet him, Mom?" She hates being called "Mom" because she's not your mom—she's your baby's mom.

WATCH FOR SIGNS OF EXHAUSTION. One buddy, trying not to wake up his wife and their baby, quietly brushed his teeth in a darkened bathroom—and accidentally brushed with his baby's diaper ointment! He then woke up not only his wife but his dentist (when he called him to find out how you get that greasy stuff off your teeth and gums).

The baby slept through the entire ordeal.

---

45. If you feel shell-shocked by tiredness, you're in good company.

My buddies described early fatherhood fatigue as "just horrible" or "like torture" or "truly grueling . . . unlike anything I'd ever experienced." So what do you do?

Temporarily cut out extraneous activities. My friend Jeff said, "I couldn't see straight, so I cut. Reading the paper—gone! Tennis twice a week—gone! Phone calls to insignificant friends—gone!"

And don't waste your energy by constantly complaining. One friend said he and his wife accidentally fell into complaining matches. "It was like we were in a bizarre competition: who was most tired. What a worthless exercise!"

Fatherhood sometimes seems like a series of goal-line stands. If it helps, tack a picture of Bart Starr's famous quarterback sneak to the inside of your clothes closet (beside your chore list).

46. Become a master of the afternoon nap.

Whenever you have an opportunity, unplug your phone, lie down on a couch or on the floor, set an alarm, and totally zonk out. After a nap, you'll sometimes feel as though you had a full night's sleep.

Until you get your sleep back, remember to look both ways before you cross the street and double-check that you've got your keys, turned off the stove, and written everything down in your date book. Don't end up at the police station reporting your lost wallet; your time is better spent with your wife and baby.

DON'T FORGET TO LAUGH.

---

47. Have fun.

The biggest problem with fatherhood is that we keep our expectations too low. Bust through those constraints and let your baby bring out the kid in you.

48. Show your baby the world.

Every home is different, but in ours, I adventured. My wife nurtured. My kids learned early on: Daddy likes active time; Mommy likes quiet time. Even if the roles are reversed in your situation, don't miss the opportunity to go out with your baby—just the two of you. Think of these outings as a new sport you've taken up. Like any sport, you need to be outfitted. Get a front-style pack and a backpack. If you run or blade, get a baby jogger. If you bike, get a baby bike trailer.

Some days after we returned from the hospital, I took to the street with our brand-new baby in a front-style pack. At the first street corner, a golden retriever glided past, shimmering in the morning sun. My son took note (or I imagined he did) and made some squabbling noises, and I said, "Let's see your first golden retriever." The owner said her dog was great with babies, so I lowered my son. I knew he could only focus on objects about a foot away. Face to face, he seemed entranced: his first doggie breath. His first wagging tail. His first slobbering lick (no, I didn't let *that* happen—it would be like dropping him in the most polluted spot of the Ganges).

As we walked away, I thought, *all these firsts.* First tree. First traffic signal. First newsstand—well, I skipped that one. (Too many firsts there!)

49. Who cares what others think of you?

You'll be at the vegetable market selecting a melon when your baby goes into a crying fit. You accidentally elbow the melon display, and dozens of melons hit the deck and roll down the aisles. Yikes! You try to collect the rolling fruit and calm your baby, but bending over pushes your baby's panic button. Her screams drown out the "Sale on Cracker Barrel cheese, aisle five," announcement on the intercom. All the other shoppers shake their heads in unison: *Incompetent father wipes out again.*

So what?! Pick up the melons and move on.

50. Don't dress your baby boy in pink.

You can dress your baby girl in any color you want, but if you dress your baby boy with even a touch of pink, you practically have to show the world his penis to convince them that he's male. Sorry—that's the way it is.

51. Write a will, choose guardians, buy insurance, and meet with a financial advisor.

Right: Your forehead gets sweaty just thinking about it, because these obligations underscore the fact that yes, even you *will one day die.* That's why they're necessary, so don't stall anymore if you haven't gotten around to doing anything. (I procrastinated so long I had to have our lawyer fax our will to us minutes before we were supposed to go on vacation, reams of pages spilling onto the floor, the taxi honking outside our door.) You owe it to your wife and kid (and both of you owe it to your baby) to ensure a reasonable future if you're not around.

Call a business-savvy friend and ask for the name of a lawyer. Meet with the lawyer in person, be sure you're comfortable, discuss hourly rates, and get an estimate in writing for the estate planning. He's going to ask you and your wife a lot of nosy questions. Relax—it's necessary information. Our lawyer looked me in the eye and said, "You die. Your wife has to bring up your baby. Now, how does she manage?" I practically needed smelling salts—but these questions prompt financial plans.

On the financial-planning front, college seems a long way away, but by the time you have to start paying tuition, the projected cost of a four-year education could hover around $200,000, including room, board, and beer. Start and *maintain* some kind of savings plan now.

LAST WARNING: NOTIFY YOUR INSURANCE AGENT! You've got thirty days after the birth to get your baby on your health insurance plan. If, God forbid, your baby were to get sick and needed hospitalization, you wouldn't want it to break you financially, too (your heart will already be broken). No excuses! Call now!

Then, always keep your insurance card in your wallet. You never know when you'll have to rush your baby to an emergency room.

---

52. Find the right pediatrician.

Most likely, you interviewed and selected your pediatrician weeks before the baby's birth. And here's what you looked for: the tone in his responses; his medical ideology; his payment and fee schedule; his office location, hours, and ambience; his medical degrees and hospital affiliation; and his ability to return phone calls. You probably chose the pediatrician who came highly recommended from friends and hoped for the best.

We selected a gray-haired pediatrician with a soft, even voice, a nice-but-not-flashy style, and a wall that could barely contain his degrees from top universities. But almost immediately, we questioned if he was right for us. We were jarred by his baby handling during the routine first inspection at the hospital. He seemed irritated by our questions. His secretary put us on hold whenever we called. Our pharmacist rolled his eyes and complained of delays. Then the doctor made a hasty medical judgment that would have proved dangerous to our child's well-being had we not trusted our instinct and brought her to an emergency room. Fired! The relationship with your pediatrician is based on trust, so the instant you begin to question his decisions, it's time to move on.

53. Know what to expect at the pediatrician's office.

You open the front door and there will be a logjam of baby strollers. You'll jostle some out of the way to make space for your baby's stroller, then you'll go into the germ-clogged waiting room. There will be toys that are so mouthed and fondled you'll wonder how they can be sanitary. Then: the wait. Almost immediately, I'd begin tapping my knee and hyperventilating and looking at my watch and asking the receptionist if she had any idea how much longer we'd be waiting. "Chill," my wife would say (but she's capable of waiting two hours without splitting a gut). Then a truly sick kid would leave with a frazzled parent, and I'd feel guilty for having been in such a rush.

Almost against my will, I found myself comparing our baby to the other babies. You might do the same. Inevitably, you'll be wondering how she measures up in terms of development. You'll balance that worry by thinking smugly to yourself that your perfect little baby will never turn out to look like the sniffling four-year-old who's banging on the wooden train in the corner—and you'll wonder how it might be to have an older child. Finally, your baby is called by her name and you feel a glee in knowing someone else recognizes your baby as a separate entity from you.

All the horror of your own pediatrician visits comes back to you in a flash. At first, your baby looks on with great curiosity while the doctor weighs her or measures her height or puts the stethoscope to her chest. Then she thinks, *Should I cry? Yes!* Once she starts, the office visit resembles an Indy car in a pit stop: a series of checks, all above the roar of the engine. Amazingly, the pediatrician will talk in a steady voice, offering occasional consolation to the baby, and you don't know who you feel sorry for most: your baby, yourself, or the doctor. *How could anyone do this day in, day out?*

Now comes the reason you're there: questions. Write a list before your baby's visit or, invariably, you'll forget the most important query. Prioritize your questions. Be sure to bring any notes you've made on your baby's condition, with dates, times, and symptoms. Your baby's pediatrician sees his share of frazzled parents, and you don't want to be one of them.

On your way out, thank everyone—especially the nurses and desk attendants. These people are your lifeline to the doctor and will fit your sick baby into the doctor's busy schedule more readily if they feel you appreciate their efforts.

54. *Some pediatrician visits will seem unnecessary.*

Here's what will happen to you: Your baby cries when you set him down and you wonder if it's an ear infection, or your infant has a high fever and your wife read something about some obscure disease in her baby book. You call your doctor; he tells you to bring the baby in; he takes a quick look and says, "Nothing much to worry about. Let's keep an eye on him."

Naturally, you're thrilled he's okay, but the ordeal has you blitzed. You had a struggle to get him out of the house and into the doctor's office, you waited half an hour (or an hour and a half) in the waiting room, you're out a morning of work, you've got a whopping bill to pay, and you're trying to tell yourself, "Well, we did the right thing by bringing him in."

Remember that your peace of mind is worth something, and what's wrong with trying to protect your child against serious illness or injury? Besides, few doctors will make judgments based on your amateur descriptions of symptoms, so try not to feel suckered when the doctor says he won't prescribe a medication without seeing your child.

And don't get angry at your wife if she's the one who insisted on bringing your baby to the doctor. It was awfully taxing for her, too. Turn the whole thing around by bringing her flowers.

55. *No two babies react to the doctor the same way.*

Our daughter screamed until her screams were silent. Our son calmly studied the doctor's every move as though he were a medical student. Some things are built into your kid—and there's little you can do to change them.

56. When a doctor tells you not to worry, don't worry.

Just as in pregnancy, the rule is, "Don't worry until there's something to worry about." Even when you get a bad result, stay calm and get second and third medical opinions.

BUY A MIST VAPORIZER FOR THE NURSERY. Your wife will love you for it, because she's concerned about the air going into your baby's lungs. We turned ours on for the entire winter, and the warm mist helped comfort our baby (especially when she had a cold or cough). When the air in the room gets thick with humidity, you can play a rain forest tape and pretend you're floating down the Amazon.

---

57. You will realize all those wee-hour calls to your wife's obstetrician were merely training for wee-hour calls to your baby's pediatrician.

Don't worry: Your pediatrician expects frequent calls from you, especially if you and your wife are first-time parents. Get up the nerve, lift the phone, dial. Of course, cloak your frantic question in a profuse apology, then empty all the worries from your mind in one call. Start with the first symptoms, then describe the precise times the symptoms changed. Stay exact in your descriptions and don't blabber about your second-guessing or parental self-doubts.

With an infant, you should call any time there's a high fever or you detect unusual symptoms. In due course, you'll become more proficient at knowing when to call and at recounting in pseudomedical terminology whatever is ailing your child.

58. All right, it's been four weeks and you're getting tired of the cold shoulder.

One new father said, "During those first few weeks, I felt like I should propose to my hand!"

Yes, your wife knows what's going on. My friend Paula said, "One day, I was putting away some shirts when I noticed these rolled-up porno magazines in my husband's sports jacket pockets. Since he never before had any interest in that, I said, 'Honey, is there something we ought to be talking about here?' He blushed and I realized I'd best not check his sports coat pockets for a while."

Remember to be extra considerate of your wife's feelings or she might say something like, "You didn't just get eight stitches in the crotch!"

59. Now that one month has passed, have a small celebration.

When your baby's asleep, prop your wife's feet on pillows, stick a video of a recent movie you both missed in the VCR, hand her a bowl of popcorn or ice cream, and snuggle. You both need a reprieve, so take it. Without pauses, early parenthood can seem like a hundred-hour workweek.

60. In the midst of all the things that seem to be going wrong, don't forget to talk with your wife about all the things that are going right.

One might be your coordination with your wife. When our infant son got sick, we took turns walking him through the night in two-hour shifts. During one changing of the guard, I threw my arm around my wife and said, "You're so beautiful." She shot me a look: *Liar.* "Hey," I said, "if we're not snapping each other's heads off right now, that means . . . well, it means . . . "

"I know exactly what you're saying," she said, kissing me. "And now, I'm going to sleep."

61. Don't get arrogant when the going is good.

There will be moments when everything seems dandy. Your wife is brimming with confidence, she fits into her favorite suit (but not into her favorite jeans yet), and she likes nursing. And you're thinking of saying to your wife, "Having a baby is *fabulous.* And you know what? We're not half bad as parents. Sure, we took a few knocks, but we're surviving. Let's just enjoy this."

Don't say a word. I can't explain it, but the second you do, the gods hit your baby with teething or an ear infection or a high fever—and you're reeling again. Know how a baseball player keeps mum when he's on a tear? It's more than just good form; it's a combination of superstition and reverence for the powers that be. Same with fatherhood.

2.

CRIB DAYS:
Two to Six Months

62. Gentlemen, set your watches, please.

Can you believe four weeks have passed? Doesn't it seem like only yesterday when you and your wife brought home a tiny infant? (Judging by the bags under your eyes, it doesn't *look* like only a month . . . just kidding.)

Well, fasten your seat belts, because it's going to take off from here. Months will whip by like calendar pages flying off the screen in a 1940s movie. You learn to grasp on to moments like they were handholds on the slippery rock of fatherhood . . . or you feel like you're free-falling through time zones. It might be the lazy afternoon pushing your baby in a swing or it might be the first time she sits up, but you'll need markers or the trail will feel blurred.

Time to give yourself a pat on the back. You're doing great. And you are (despite all your hyperventilating) feeling like a father. Right?

63. Bring your baby into your bed in the morning to cuddle.

Just the three of you in bed, a love sandwich, with the smells of wife and baby and smooth skin and later little feet kicking against a white sheet . . . Guys, this is as good as it gets. Let it sink in.

But, a warning: Try not to let these visits creep up any earlier than, say, seven A.M. What's tricky, of course, is that the baby loves this bed-cuddling so much that invariably it gets pushed closer to six-thirty, then six, then five-thirty, until you're so cranky from the lack of sleep you threaten to outlaw early-morning cuddling altogether. Stick to a time so you don't end up blowing your fuse.

64. But treat your bed as sacred ground.

Just after our daughter was born, a wise friend said, "I'll give you just one bit of wisdom: Keep your bed as yours and your wife's." He made me promise I'd set limits on our bed.

Well . . . it didn't quite work out that way. My wife adored the Cave Family sense of everyone tumbling around on the same mattress. "We're being so Western Industrialist," she argued. (I held back from saying, "But we *are* Western Industrialist.") Great: She could literally sleep with our baby stretched out over her face. I, on the other hand, woke with every rustle. I'd jolt awake, sweaty and hysterical, sure that I had rolled over our baby. I'd yell *Haaa!* and throw the pillows from the bed in a desperate attempt to save the baby I was sure I'd crushed. "Not again," my wife would groan. I looked a decade older every morning. People stopped me on the street. "You look like shit." *Gee . . . thanks!* "No, I mean it: You *really* look like shit!"

But the worst part was that we'd let our baby figure out that our spacious bed with the down comforter, the pile of pillows, and two warm bodies on either side was a far more attractive option than her crib, with its cheap mattress and prisonlike bars. At 2:23 A.M., our baby would be screaming and we'd have a choice: Pull a pillow over our heads and try to sleep through the ruckus, or get instant quiet by retrieving our baby. Invariably, we opted for the latter.

Big mistake. After a few weeks, she was hooked. Unfortunately, family bed addiction isn't an easy habit to kick. Slowly, we taught her to tolerate her crib. (The method: Comfort your baby in the crib, leave the room, let her cry, go back in due time, comfort some more, leave. After several nights, progress: You sleep during the days. Finally, you get your bed back.)

Look, we blew it badly with the bed business and all three of us survived. The important thing to know with all these issues is that if you've made a minor mistake in parenting, it's not a crisis. You just need to make a course correction.

BUY A BIGGER BED. Your wife's back is still killing her from late pregnancy. Your baby has become instantly addicted to cuddling, and you need more prime real estate or you'll be falling on the floor. Sure, the last thing you need is another expense, but if you can, splurge.

I did . . . and at the bed showroom, I actually fell asleep on a mattress when the salesperson walked away to help another customer. Minutes later, he nudged me awake. "Any chance you can ship me on it?" I asked feebly.

P.S. While you're at it, buy her new sheets or a comforter. (She knows the gift is for her, since you could care less!) It's a marriage revitalizer.

---

65. Don't look at the crib as if it's a maximum-security prison.

No, I didn't want our baby in our bed. Yes, I wanted her in her crib. But it wasn't until I'd done some interior decorating in our baby's crib that I felt it was acceptable. A mirror here, a mobile there (with a windup music center), a few squeaky toys, some plastic books, one of the zillion rattles friends gave us, one of the zillion teething rings that our extended family gave us, and voila!

I didn't feel completely content until our baby discovered "her corner," where she'd jam her head against the bumpers, pull her arms under her body (like a bird huddling in a nest), and wear a contented, secure, asleep expression—an expression that said, *Daddy, you can take it easy now.*

66. Use your exhaustion as a sign to let your baby cry during the night.

Eventually, you'll be so worn and downtrodden that you won't respond to your baby's nighttime cries. Good. This is nature's way of making you get real. Sure, if there's a distress cry, respond immediately (and be sure there's no fever or illness). But your baby needs to know how to comfort herself, and if you take every cry to heart, she'll never figure out how to do that.

67. It's okay to be schmaltzy.

Croon to your baby. She'll be looking into your eyes with that lopsided, toothless grin and you'll feel like the most charming guy around. (Don't you wish you were half as amazing as you are in your baby's eyes?)

It's an obvious thing to do, but you'd be surprised how many men withhold displays of affection from their kids because they're afraid of going all gooey. Be man enough to be sentimental.

MAKE PLASTER CASTS OF YOUR BABY'S HANDS AND FEET. You can try it yourself (buy a kit and follow the instructions). Or hire a pro, who will wait until your baby is asleep, make the negative casts of those incredibly tiny hands and feet, and return days later with . . . art.

This gift will be a major hit with your wife. Decline if the artisan offers to paint the casts in flesh tone (tacky). Place the casts high on a shelf, somewhere safe from your future toddler.

68. If your baby is so marvelous, why is work suddenly so alluring?

"I can't explain why," my friend Brad said, "but once I got my wife and our baby home, I couldn't wait to bury myself in work. I could immerse myself totally in a way I never could before. It was almost scary." His wife was terrified, too. "I was thrilled that he took providing so seriously," she said. "We needed the cash. But I felt abandoned. I had serious postpartum blues, the house was held together by Scotch tape, and I felt he was off at work in total peace and quiet. I know he was using work as an excuse."

But it's not only you who finds work a reprieve from the early home madness. My friend Monique said, "I couldn't handle being home with a baby. I was bored. Frustrated. I missed being in the world. I missed the recognition of doing something. I missed coworkers and assignments and wearing a skirt or a dress or a suit. All in all, early motherhood was drudgery in comparison to work." You may even want to consider Monique's solution: she went to work and her husband stayed home with their baby.

Remember, those are serious issues for the two of you. Dust off your communication skills and seek resolutions and compromises.

69. Help your wife through work guilt.

She's hearing a lot of conflicting comments: "You're staying at home with the baby?" "Don't you find it boring just being a homemaker?" "You're going back to work so soon?" "Aren't you worried about leaving a little baby with a stranger?" "Don't you realize this is the formative period for your child?" And on and on. No wonder she's feeling guilty. She goes back to work and she's a bad mother. She stays home and she's not ambitious. She does both and maybe she won't be good at either. She can't win!

This is tricky stuff for you, too. Maybe her career is just as serious as yours. Maybe you hoped for her income to help out, too. On the other hand, if she stays home full time, does she seem, well, more banal when she doesn't have a day's worth of work events to report?

It's your job to help her sift through what other people (including you) expect of her and what she wants for herself. Be a good sounding board. Help her find the right balance.

70. Never, ever say your work is more important than your wife's mothering and housework.

Don't say to your wife, "But I'm the one who's working!" Try to understand that her job is never finished, your baby's nap is never long enough, and your wife often feels (perhaps for the first time) like a failure.

Instead, say, "You've had a tough day, so let me watch the baby while you take a break." If it's six P.M. and she still hasn't had a chance to take her morning shower, she needs your help—now!

71. Don't blame your wife when your baby goes bonkers at the witching hour (early evening—when all hell breaks loose and the pictures on your walls vibrate from your baby's screams).

Sometimes, everything's fine until you walk in the door. This is especially rough on fathers, because it seems your baby is going wild *because* of you. It's not what you envisioned. You want to feel like a noble knight returning to the castle after slaying dragons. You want a kiss from the fair lady. You want a gurgle from the little heir to the kingdom. You don't actually need trumpeting horns, but a cold beer, a hot shower, and a moment's peace would be great. Then, you hope the baby will zonk out in the crib and you'll get to go to bed with the fair lady.

Instead, your wife shoots you a sarcastic *the-cavalry's-arrived-in-the-nick-of-time* look. It's bedlam. High decibels, raging tempers, complete chaos. "Here! Take him!" she says, thrusting the screaming baby at you, and throwing herself on the bed sobbing.

Careful now. Blow this and the entire evening is down the tubes. Never blame your wife for the bedlam. Things might have been perfect before you walked in—which doesn't necessarily mean you've triggered the blowup. Often, it's just how it worked out.

Place your ear to the door before going in. Hear anything? If you hear a hysterical baby inside, don't flee. Breathe deeply. Focus on the positive, and walk in. Purge your mind of work. Your first words are the most important. Never talk about your day right away. Ask about her day and your baby's day. Let her know you appreciate the stress she's under. Devise a plan to arrest the negative momentum and create a special night.

P.S. Don't tank up on booze before the witching hour; it only makes it easier to have an argument.

---

10 THINGS YOUR WIFE LIKES TO HEAR WHEN YOU COME HOME FROM WORK:

1. "I really missed you two."
2. "I can't believe how well you're handling all this."
3. "It's my shift. Your turn to chill."
4. "I'm taking the baby out to the bookstore."
5. "Here's dinner!"
6. "These flowers are for you."
7. "Tell me about your day."
8. "I'm taping the ball game. Let's take the baby for a stroll."
9. "The baby's asleep? Let's make dinner together like we used to."
10. "I saw this in a store window and thought it would look great on you. Go try it on!"

---

72. Remember, if you come home after work and blow the whole "Daddy's home!" entrance by starting a fight, you should walk out, come back in, and start over.

73. Eat together with your wife.

The tendency is to scarf down food separately, while the other watches the baby. Don't. Put your baby in a bouncy chair, pour a glass of wine for you and for your wife, and try to keep your meals fun and romantic. If you don't eat together, you miss a vital connection.

74. Don't always use TV and video as the Baby-Sitter from Heaven.

It's very tempting (and almost every new parent will give in sometimes). You start rationalizing: "Well, it's *Big Bird in China,* so it's educational." Or, "You can't get any more musical than *Sing Along Songs.*" Problem is, while you're having your quiet time, your baby is learning to zone out. It's an ugly pattern.

Years later, you'll walk into a room and your kid will have a cornflake glued to his chin, his spoon poised an inch off his mouth, and he'll be frozen, eyes to TV. "Hello? Hello?" You wave your hand before his face. No response (he's enjoying a TV photon blast). And it all started way back when . . .

75. Expect constant interruptions.

Meals and conversations will not flow as they had, so be prepared to start-stop-start-stop your vivid tale that you really wanted to tell your wife *now*! When there's truly something that has to be told in one go, save it for when your child is asleep.

76. Prepare to be forgetful.

We were riding in a taxi one evening when I said to my wife, "I know we're going to a dinner party but I've got no idea whose party it is." My wife tilted her head, as if to say, *Man, you're losing it!* Well, maybe I am. I've left shirts at the Laundromat for a year, left pots on the stove until they burned, believed my glasses were lost once a day. But nothing so bad as what happened to my friend Nico, who left a bath running while he went downstairs and didn't realize what he'd done until he destroyed his newly renovated home. My theory: There's only so much room in your noggin—and your baby pushes you over the limit.

I've discovered ways to control my absentmindedness. I now set everything in one spot: my glasses here, my wallet there, my keys here. I also learned that my former skill at muddling my way through a storm of disarray didn't work once I was a father. Which is why I've found it even more important than before to write everything down in an orderly fashion, check things off my daily calendar, and at week's end, double-check what I've done.

77. Watch for signs of stress.

A few months into fatherhood, I went to my dentist, who told me I'd better get a dental night guard or I'd be eating nothing but mashed potatoes by the time my kid was in college. "Have you noticed how you're grinding your teeth when you sleep?" she asked. "*What* sleep?" I said.

If you see signs of stress, do something about it. Then try to reduce the stress by creating breaks where you do nothing, as in deep-breathing or a five-minute walk.

78. Be prepared to hear The Voice.

Your mouth will be moving, but the words, the tone, the content won't be yours. Whose voice is it? It's your father's. And what a jolt! Fatherhood has brought you one giant step closer to being your dad.

Terrific if you're a big fan of your father's fathering and you find yourself saying the right thing almost instinctively. Not so great if you weren't and you end up parroting someone else's malicious snipes. Some of my buddies reported saying things like, "Can't you please shut him up?" or "I've got work to do!" or "Get me out of here!" or "It's not my problem!"

You don't like how it sounds? Well, neither does your wife. Immediately backtrack, apologize, and think. Then say what *you* really mean.

79. Dream of your baby's future.

I was lying on the bed, too zonked to sleep, afraid to move. After two hours of crying, the baby had finally succumbed to slumber. She had a fist near each of my ears and she was breathing on my chin.

Suddenly, though, I flashed to the way things were, back in the old days of freedom. Before I met my wife, I used to save up some cash and take off to Europe in August. I'd buy a Eurail pass and flit from city to city without a plan. One of my money-saving schemes was to hop a train—any train—at midnight, set my alarm for four A.M., get off, and take the next train back to the city of my departure. Free hotel! And if I slept through, well, I'd just go to another destination, whatever that may be. Now, with my baby pressed to my chest, with her heart beating into mine, I wondered when, if ever, I'd wing it like that again.

I began to long for the good ol' days, when another image flashed before my eyes: Someday, I'd hit the trains of Europe with my wife and daughter. And then an even more vivid image came to mind: My college-age daughter would ask if we would visit her during her junior year abroad. We'd meet her boyfriend. Naturally, he'd have a charming accent and his eyes would glitter whenever he looked toward her. Whew. I guessed I'd be ready for it when the time came.

A baby sets off what came before from everything that will happen later. It's okay; it's part of the whole dad thing.

LAUGH AT YOURSELF WHEN YOU START THINKING, WHO COULD* POSSIBLY *BE GOOD ENOUGH FOR MY LITTLE GIRL? You start envisioning yourself walking twenty paces behind your teenage girl. "Don't you dare!" you'll be yelling, shaking a baseball bat at potential courtiers. And she's still a baby.

Don't worry—you're not alone. Every new dad feels protective of his baby girl. Fortunately, you've got time to acclimate.

---

80. Fight your instinct to flee.

Whenever our baby would cry endlessly, I'd whine to my wife, "Get me to India." "India?" she'd reply. "That's right, India," I'd retort. "I always wanted to go to India. And right this minute, I really want to go." "Why the hell does he want to go to *India?*" she'd ask the wall.

To flee, that's why—and to me, India's the farthest place to flee to. No phone, no fax, no e-mail where I'd go, and no crying babies either (none that are mine, anyway). We guys want it *all.* When I asked my buddies if they dreamed of far-off lands, nearly everyone said, "Oh, yeah." My friend Larry said, "I suddenly had an urge to get my pilot's license. My wife said, 'Well, isn't this transparent!' We fought, I got the license anyway, I flew for two years, then realized I had no need to escape. I realized I loved being a father. Everything paled beside being home with my wife and our baby."

I never made it to India, but I did, a year after our son was born, take a six-day pseudo-work vacation to Italy. Funny thing was, I'd be eating pizza and having a beer at an outdoor restaurant, watching Italian families walk back and forth, licking gelato and chirping operatically, and I'd suddenly wish I was chasing my kids around the piazza. I'd yank out a family photo, stare at it, and feel my chest tighten. Then I'd call home and they'd be out, and I'd imagine they were having a better time than me.

81. Temper your fear of commitment.

Right: some of us stammered through, "Will you m-m-ma-rrrry m-m-me?" and then hemmed and hawed about having a baby while our wife begged us to "grow up." Why? For the same reason we stop at the video return pile—even though we've got exactly the video we want for the night, *what if there's something better?*

Fear of commitment is not easily resolved. Ask other guys how they conquered their conflict and they'll talk about "the click." My friend Jeffrey said, "I was lying on an operating table before surgery and I felt a little click. Suddenly, I was no longer scared of commitment." Another friend said, "My wife got sick and I realized I could never lose her. There was a click . . . " For me, I heard "the click" while lying in a mud bath with my wife, and we were engaged within a month.

It's the same with fatherhood. You get sick or your wife does or your baby does, and you think, *How could I exist without my family?* Or there's a moment of clarity: You and your child are catching snowflakes in your mouths while you're ice skating and you realize it's one of the great moments of your life. There's a click.

Sometimes it helps to ask your wife how she deals with *her* fears of commitment. I asked my wife why new mothers in general don't seem as flipped out by the new-parent madness as do new fathers. She said, "Lots of men don't understand that life is made up of little moments and that's all there is in the end and you'd better be happy with it. This baby's going to give us plenty of little moments."

She was right. The next time you feel yourself freeze while your crying, sucking, cooing, farting little creature flails her arms, say to yourself, *It's not always going to be as rough.* Or listen to Janis belt out, *Freedom's just another word for nothin' left to lose.* Sure, you realize how much you suddenly have to lose: Adding a child to a divorce is like adding nuclear arms to a war.

Here's the catch-22 of fatherhood: You can't just dip your toe into fatherhood or you never reap the rewards. So jump in with both feet. If you do, your fears of commitment will begin to vanish.

82. Listen to your wife—don't shave your head.

You may be so preoccupied with your wife and baby you may not realize how nutty you've gotten. But your wife will have enough sense left to straighten you out, if need be.

One night, I felt so fried I said to my wife, "I think I'm going to shave my head." She looked at me and asked, "Why?" "Because I'm losing my hair and I read that the ancient Chinese used to shave their heads in order to stimulate hair growth and I can't bear the thought of not having hair."

"Let me get this straight," she said. "You want to shave your head so you'll have no hair because you're afraid of having no hair?" I had trouble explaining it. "Go to sleep," she said. I did.

When I woke up, I decided to grow a beard instead, which looked scraggly and needed more maintenance than shaving and got tugged on incessantly by our baby's clutching fingers, but was the perfect expression of my muddled state of mind.

83. Don't hide on the golf course.

Ask ten mothers what they hate most about fatherhood and six will say, "Golf." I never tried golf for the same reason I never tried heroin: What if I liked it? It might be damned hard to stop. But if you already play golf, think moderation. Nine holes instead of eighteen. You get the picture.

84. Don't hide behind your lawnmower.

When your whole life goes haywire, there's nothing like jamming a cigar in your mouth, a baseball cap on your head, earphones over your ears, and taking it out on innocent blades of grass. The whole idea, as I understand it, is to make yourself so utterly unattractive that nobody will come anywhere near you. (I know firsthand: I'm guilty of this one.)

Don't overdo the lawn-as-cover business. My buddy Antoine became so obsessed when an August heat wave turned his lawn brown that he couldn't sleep and staggered out to water his yard at three A.M., leaving his wife to deal with their baby. Not the way to your wife's heart . . .

LET'S FACE IT: SIX WEEKS INTO FATHERHOOD, YOU'RE NOT THINKING ABOUT WHETHER THE BABY IS PRECISELY MEETING DEVELOPMENTAL EXPECTATIONS AND CAN HOLD HIS HEAD AT A FORTY-FIVE-DEGREE ANGLE WHEN LYING ON HIS TUMMY. You're thinking it's about time to get back to s-e-x.

85. Wait a full six weeks before you open negotiations about resuming sex with your wife.

Just between us guys, a lot of our grumbling and groaning about the Six-Week-Wait-for-Sex-to-Resume is just for show, to let our partner know how deprived we've been. We puff our chests and act pretty much like those exotic South American birds in *National Geographic* specials—you know, the ones who try desperately to attract some female attention. (Of course most of the time we've been too pooped to do anything but fall into snory slumber.) But what a show!

86. Is everything the same down there?

It all depends on the type of birth: Was there a C-section? An episiotomy? Most women will say it can take six months to a year for their bodies to heal sexually.

My buddy Charlie said, "The first time we tried sex after the delivery was a complete wipeout. We were both hot to trot, but once I was inside her, she appeared to be having about as much fun as if I were poking her with needles. I withdrew, and we rubbed each other and ourselves until we came. Then we lay there, totally dejected. Later, we talked things over and decided to give it a try in a few weeks. I'm glad we waited. The second time went much smoother. Soon thereafter, we had our momentum back."

No, the wait is not going to be fun for either of you. You've both got the nagging worry that it will *never* be the same. Then there are the wounded feelings, the sense of rejection or frustration. But you can make it worse by trying again too soon.

Know what to expect so you're not surprised. She might be drier than usual and then might suddenly become wetter than usual. Then comes the part a guy really hates: Her muscles might suddenly let go, so you feel as if the friendly confines of Wrigley Field have given way to the immensity of the Astrodome. You have no power to move her. You're slipping around. You worry she's faking her pleasure. She fears she's not satisfying you. You know you had an orgasm, but did she? Afterwards you fall on the pillow, stare at the ceiling, and wonder if your sex life is ruined forever. You both sulk.

Know that the pelvic floor is a muscle that can, like any muscle, be toned. My friend Lena, who is a physical therapist, told me, "The pelvic floor is a hammock of muscles that suspend the bladder, uterus, and rectum. During pregnancy, it gets stretched, squished—" "Stop, stop, stop, stop, stop!" I said. "I don't want to think of my wife that way. It's like hearing that my wife has a 'mucous plug.' " Then, without going into gory details, Lena said there are new biofeedback instruments and other nifty pelvic floor rehabilitation techniques that are commonplace in Europe but just making their appearance in the U.S.

Encourage your wife to do those pelvic-floor-tightening Kegel exercises or to speak with a physical therapist if it's really bothering you or her. (But remind her that you want to maintain the mystery of her body.)

87. Return to contraception.

Admit it: Making love with the intent of creating a baby was a pretty profound experience. Your wife may have broken down in tears when she sensed you had conceived. You may have, without knowing it, redefined how you view your role in the grand scheme of life.

As you get back to the basics of contraception, you might feel let down. Or your wife might. Be sure your wife consults her gynecologist for a new diaphragm fitting or gets a new prescription for birth control pills. Don't trust nursing as a birth control method. (Who thinks up these old wives' tales? The same people who brought us the rhythm method?)

Before you left the hospital, didn't one of the nurses say, "I don't want to see you back here in nine months—unless that's what you want!"?

88. Return to the missionary!

Okay, it's the third month, say, and you're having sex again. Congratulations! Time to find the right positions. You haven't used the missionary position since the pregnancy began. The weight of the baby-to-be made it both uncomfortable for your wife and potentially dangerous for her and the baby-to-be (the blood flow through her arteries was slowed).

Now, it's back. And so is a freedom you probably haven't felt in some time. Late in pregnancy, most guys feel restricted by the "thereness" of the baby. (Can the baby sense your penis? Will you accidentally initiate labor?) Sex then was more of an expression of love than a dance in bed. Time to explore your new freedom—but stay closely aware of your wife's emotional and physical tenderness.

She might not resume having orgasms immediately. If not, don't interrogate her. Maybe she has the same liftoff from her internal rockets, and maybe not. After the long wait for sex after delivery, you want to show her you're still patient.

89. Don't wake your wife up at two A.M. to have sex.

In the old days, you'd begin by nibbling kisses on her neck or . . . wherever, and, as she slowly awakened, she'd begin to moan with pleasure, run her fingers through your hair, and gyrate her body. Dreamily, you'd make love, one of you half asleep; then you'd drift off to blissful sleep again.

Those days are gone. But before you *know* they're gone, you'll try (at least once) to wake your wife for sex. Here's what you'll hear; "Are you insane?! Do you think I'd trade one wink of sleep for sex?! If you don't stop, I'm calling 911!"

90. Don't think you can treat your wife like she's been a major irritation all day or blow up about her mothering and then expect to hop into bed and make wild love.

Remember the days when you used to argue like crazy until ten P.M., dash out the house, stomp around until your anger subsided, get back at midnight, make up tearfully, and then have the greatest sex of your life until three A.M.? Well, those days are over.

You and your wife will have to develop techniques of your own to keep the zip in your sex life while all hell breaks loose in your home. One friend said, "You have to learn to separate your life as parents from your life as a couple. After the baby is asleep, get flirtatous. Act in love. Be intimate. Turn off the TV, which is sure to wreck the mood. It's all about keeping your bedroom beautiful." My friend Annette said, "I tell my husband to forget the notion of marriage totally. It's too scary. Don't think of the future. Live in the day. Never go to bed mad at one another. And if sex is not on your mind, it's not going to happen." My friend Rick said that he and his wife play a game of backgammon after the baby falls asleep, which helps remind them of the old days of courting. Another friend said he was always too wiped out after getting the baby down for the night, so he started taking his lunch-break at home to make love.

When things go haywire with the baby, try turning it into a joke; it sometimes helps keep the spark between you and your wife.

91. Don't listen to the soothsayers.

One chorus will tell you, "The first three (or six, twelve, eighteen) months are the hardest." The other camp says, "It only gets more complex." Here's the simple truth: You'll adjust! (If it's stasis or sameness you were after, well, you're in the wrong place.)

92. Dump all your useless friends.

As a new father, you simply don't have the time for friendships that stagger along like wounded soldiers.

One guy I used to know stands out in my mind as prototypical dead-wood. When we were both bachelors, we had something to talk about, but once I became a father, the conversation fizzled. His constant complaining about women he was (or wasn't) sleeping with was a total snooze. I tired of his bragging about his whopping business deals, too.

When you realize there's nothing there, don't try to rationalize it. Just let it go.

93. Ask other fathers for advice.

It's staggering how much information new mothers get from other mothers. So, why shouldn't new fathers do the same? When you need advice, pick up the phone and call a father you respect.

YOU'LL BE SPENDING MORE TIME WITH YOUR BABY THAN WITH FRIENDS. One day, a friend you used to see all the time will say, "I thought you'd dropped off the face of the earth!" (Your wife and baby know where you are.)

---

94. If they're interested, let your childless friends play indulgent aunt and uncle roles.

Some childless friends or couples you know may start doting on your kid. Let them—it's a chance for them to have a taste of what it's like to have children (without, of course, the constancy). These people make terrific, caring friends, and maybe even baby-sitters (and they frequently bring chocolate when they visit).

P.S. Be especially sensitive to single women who want a child but haven't yet had one. Yes, they're thrilled for you, but seeing you with your baby is also like pouring peroxide into their open wound.

95. Don't lose your edge.

Sometimes new fathers get overcautious. You might be tempted to stop doing anything risky. *What if something happened and you left your wife and baby alone in the world?* It's great that you're concerned, but you don't want to lose your edge, either.

It may be time for you to give up any really risky stuff—free climbing on an ice field, say. But know when to put your foot down. I'd gone to a blues joint in a dicey neighborhood of New York for as long as I could remember, but my wife questioned it after we brought our baby home. Instead of giving it up, I decided to be a little more careful. I'd go with a few friends instead of alone and leave way before closing.

Learn to compromise. If it's a weekend game of tackle football that keeps you going through the week, it would probably help if you didn't come home with a broken arm, which will severely limit your baby-holding and diaper-changing abilities. Play touch football instead.

96. Hold on to that one frivolous possession that defines you as a guy.

Maybe it's an old Stratocaster or some land where you hope to build a cabin (even if you do nothing but picnic there once a year for now) or an old sports car that has an hourly maintenance-to-drive ratio of five to one (so, it'll sit in the garage a while . . .).

If your wife doesn't completely understand your wasteful obsession, remind her it's mysteries like that that make it interesting for the two sexes to cohabitate.

97. You don't have to let your baby cramp your style.

I loved to jam our infant into the nook of my left arm and shoot jump shots with my right hand. My wife questioned the sanity of this activity. But if you're sure you won't let the ball bounce off the rim and into your baby's head, go for it. If you love to push your baby in a stroller while running or blading and know you'd never let it tip over—do it. Or if you and your wife can hit tennis balls *very softly* to one another while you hold your baby—do it.

Let your baby give you *more* style.

98. Get rid of any empathetic pregnancy weight you've put on.

I took to the gym to lose the twenty-five sympathy pounds I'd put on during my wife's pregnancy—but I soon realized that things had changed. I spotted two women in leotards staring at me. Was it my imagination or were they smiling? I sucked in my gut. I pretended to study some barbells so they could admire at will. Finally, one came over. "Excuse me," she said, "but you've got something sticking out of your T-shirt. Right here," she said, extracting a baby sock from my collar. "Uh, thanks," I mumbled.

But my real problem wasn't just the gym scene. I simply wasn't consistent in my attack on my bulging waist. One minute, I'd order an apple-celery-cucumber juice from the local health food store; then, on the way home, I'd counteract that with a bag of M&M's.

My wife continued, as she had during pregnancy, to deny she noticed any difference. "How do you explain that none of my pants fit?" I'd ask. When I looked in the mirror, it seemed to me as if I'd been dipped in a layer of wax. No muscle definition. No neck. No waist.

Here's what finally worked for me: At dawn, I ran a couple of miles, and after setting our baby down to sleep at night, I jumped rope. All those endorphins shut down my hunger and, to some extent, my eccentric eating behavior.

99. Incorporate your baby into your exercise routine.

If done carefully, your baby, in your front-style pack, is the perfect eight-pound weight for your squats, pull-ups, push-ups, knee bends, and stretches. (Not all gyms or instructors are baby-tolerant, so call in advance.) Another option: Buy exercise mats (camping insulation mats are great, too), toss on some music, and get your wife to join your living room exercise class.

Get outdoors. At the shallow end of a pool or in a shallow lake, run through the water holding your baby to your chest—great for your thighs and endurance. As your baby gets older, she'll shout, "Faster! Faster!"

ONE DAY, YOUR WIFE WILL LOOK AT THE CEILING AND YELL, "WON'T ANYBODY TAKE CARE OF ME?!" She's had it with nursing, diapers, doctors, colds, and your baby's (and your) temper tantrums. What she needs is a week off—but she's not going to get one.

Here's what you can do: Lift the phone, call your wife's best friend, tell her your wife is coming over, have your wife express milk (or help you prepare bottles with formula), tell her to dress, walk her out the door, and say you'll see her in four hours.

Do this and you'll be the rage with all your wife's friends—and certainly with your wife.

---

100. Don't get mad when your wife doesn't nap.

My friend Richard took his three-month-old daughter out for four hours so his wife could nap, but when he discovered she'd spent the time talking on the phone to friends, he lost it. "Are you crazy?" he snapped. "You're supposed to be napping! You're not supposed to be yakking!"

Oops. He spoiled the effect of his gesture and they scowled at each other the rest of the night.

101. Know your limits.

Using the suction bulb was one of mine. I thought this mini–turkey baster would suck the baby's sinuses right out of her nose. So I cravenly said to my wife, "No way. I'm not a surgeon. I don't have the nerve for it. That's your job."

You can draw the line only so often, of course. After all, your wife will have her limits, too.

102. Know how to help your baby through colic.

Want to feel helpless? Want to think you're going out of your mind? Try to console a colicky baby. It can really be hell.

Here are a few things you can try: Lay your baby over your knees, stomach down. Then, slowly circle your hand over her back. Maybe you'll get a burp that will be a more pleasant sound than Tino Martinez's grand slam against Kevin Brown in the '98 Series (assuming you're a Yankee fan). Or swaddle your baby. Or put some nice warm socks on your baby (this method defies logic, but so does colic—and you'll try anything, right?). Alter your baby's diet. Try soy or rice milk instead of cow's milk. Drive your baby around the block or turn on the radio.

The most important thing is that you and your wife are a team, so don't take snipes at one another. Call the pediatrician, spill the beans, ask for advice. Then, call the baby-sitter, offer her time and a half, get out of the house, and save your marriage. Know that after a while your baby's colic will go away.

103. Be prepared for your baby's first really serious fever.

There's nothing more terrifying than picking up a crying baby and realizing he's burning up. Fearing the worst, you grab your thermometer. If you're comfortable using a rectal thermometer, great. If you're like me (and your worst childhood nightmare was when you saw Mom or Dad waving that damned thing in the air, knowing it was headed up your butt), go out and buy an ear thermometer. Now, practice on your wife if you must, but get proficient at pulling down the ear lobe, inserting the nozzle, and pushing simultaneously. When the thermometer starts climbing from 101 to 102 to 103, you'll start running *Bonanza* reruns in your head of babies needing cold baths and doctors galloping on white horses from the nearest ranch. Don't panic (!!!). Your wife needs you to be calm, and so does your baby.

Double-check your reading, know that ear thermometers tend to run high, and don't be afraid to wake the pediatrician, even if it's 2:19 A.M. (which it will somehow *always* be).

104. Help your wife administer medications to your baby.

It takes two people (minimum!) to get any medicine in a baby's mouth. Your baby swings her head wildly or clenches her jaw to avoid the dropper and you're sweating bullets and your wife is ready to break down—and finally, after fifteen minutes of wrangling, you get a few drops down the gullet. Your shirt and hair are drenched, your arms are shaking, and you feel as if you've just gotten a saddle on a wild stallion.

Some babies, like our son, couldn't hold medicine down, so it usually ended up all over his clothes, our clothes, the car seat, the couch, or the dinner table. Be sure to ask your pediatrician about suppository medicines, which might work for your kid. Chewable tablets work for some kids, too (consider mixing the tablet in apple sauce or ice cream).

After you've succeeded (or failed) at medicating your child, your wife will at least know that you didn't shirk your responsibility in assisting her.

105. Can you believe how obsessed you are with your baby's bowel movements?

You get to know your baby's digestive tract through her facial expressions. A scrunched, red face equals constipation. As a remedy, try prune juice diluted in water. A rectal thermometer is also very effective at unstopping your baby. Later, when she's eating solid foods, feed her prunes in oatmeal or banana.

You don't need to study her face to know when she's got diarrhea. When she's on solid foods, try rice or peeled, grated apples.

Know that both constipation and diarrhea are less prevalent while your baby is breast-feeding. It gets a lot trickier to keep your baby's digestive tract in order once she's on solid foods.

106. Wash your hands frequently.

In the old sing-along TV shows, a Ping-Pong ball would bounce from word

.o word. Well, in your family, it represents a cold going from Baby ımy to Daddy to Baby to Daddy to Mommy.

Washing your hands a dozen times a day helps break the cycle. Get ıe hand cream for your wife, and rub some over your own red knuckles hen nobody's looking.

P.S. If you really want to blow your wife away, suggest she put sugar in her hand cream. Sounds crazy, but it gives her skin a (temporary) glow.

107. Get ready for the Everything-in-Baby's-Mouth Stage.

First it's the thumb. Then the toes. Then the foot. Finally, it's anything handy.

I'd brought my kids to a local stable. My daughter and I were watching the horses when I realized my son (resting over my shoulder) was actually mouthing a shelf that appeared to have two centuries of dead flies and airborne shit on it. I practically heaved. If I'd left our little prince on the ground, he would have mouthed the pointy toe on every cowboy boot in sight.

Never let your guard down!

108. Expect to hit bottom in your conversations.

One friend said, "We were sitting around one night with colds, all blowing our noses. My husband said to our two-year-old son (who can blow his own nose), 'Good one! Look what your nose made!' And I was using the nose suction bulb on our four-month-old and squirting it onto a burpee cloth to see what I'd extracted and my husband was saying to her (so she wouldn't feel left out), 'Oohhh! Great! Look what your nose made!' And I'm blowing my nose. And he's blowing his nose. And we're looking into all these tissues. Finally, I turned to him and said, 'Hey, honey, this is our family moment!' "

Don't worry; your conversations will improve. Until then, you'll sound like every other family starting out.

109. Don't blame each other.

There will be a million times you and your wife will be tempted to throw yet more verbal barbs at one another. "You were totally nuts to bring her out in that deluge, and now we're paying the price!" Don't. Both of you are making your best judgments, and mistakes are going to happen.

At no time is the incrimination game more tempting than when your baby gets sick. You forgot your baby's hat or she let your baby cook in her snowsuit or you didn't dry her hair or. . . . Careful, now, because you can create marital strife that is tougher to repair than your baby's runny nose.

But nothing will unravel you so much as your baby's crying. Know those model boats inside a bottle? You think, How did it get in there and how can it get *out*?

The experts will offer their tips, and you'll try (in no particular order): burping and making white noise by turning on the vacuum in the hallway outside the baby's room and running up and down stairs (with your baby) and bicycling your baby's legs in a frenzied attempt to extract a fart and making shadow puppets with your hands and bottle-feeding and breast-feeding and playing music and turning music off and setting the radio in between stations (more white noise) and singing and rotating the mobile and massaging and letting your baby suck your thumb and swaddling and changing the diaper and changing it again . . .

Some of these tricks work some of the time, but none of them work all of the time. Two tips. First, know that your baby's crying has a momentum. Babies test the water: a hiccup cry, a rustle, a wail, then, like a Ferrari picking up speed, they're off. Catch your baby before she's crying at ninety miles per hour. Second, don't blame your wife, because your marital fight will prompt your baby to cry at 115 miles per hour.

At the end of the day, you know you're slightly wackier than you were the day before. Maybe you've chomped off your fingernails—as I did many times during our baby's crying. Maybe you got another gray hair. But you still want to be married when the crying is over.

110. Romanticize strolling your baby.

On a gorgeous evening, stroll your baby down a tree-lined street. Ask your wife to push one side; you push the other. Then, when your baby is asleep or especially peaceful, pause, pull your wife to you, and kiss her. (And make it a real kiss—the kind you used to give her at rock concerts.)

You'll be imagining everyone you pass is admiring the most beautiful baby in the world and your wife will be thinking what a perfect family you are.

111. Keep a journal.

Nothing fancy—just scribble some notes about what's going on. Unless you do, you won't remember where you were when your baby had her first ice cream or when you finally plopped on the couch with your kid to watch *The Wizard of Oz* and sang "Follow the Yellow Brick Road."

When you fall behind (and you will), don't trash the project. Who cares if you missed writing about a game of hide-and-seek? Just pick up where you left off. Keep it handy, on the kitchen counter or on your bedside table.

P.S. You and your wife will get a kick reading all this later.

112. *Roughouse with your baby.*

My wife wasn't so sure when she saw me playfully tossing our baby up into the air or when I held her upside down. But I couldn't resist our daughter's shrieks of joy. Whenever I stopped, our baby made noises I knew to mean "More! More! More!" I was happy to oblige.

Nearly every guy I know did rough-and-tumble play with the baby while his wife shook her head or bit her fingernails. Take all the proper precautions, know there's no room for errors—then have a ball.

113. *But don't rile up your kid at bedtime.*

Daddy's home! The baby makes a fuss (or, later, gleefully charges to the door), and all semblance of domestic tranquillity that your wife has so carefully constructed for the past hour is gone. You hug your baby and swing her in a circle, growl and whoop, get down on hands and knees, romp, toss pillows at each other, and generally churn up your home. Then you spot your wife's evil eye and think, *Whatsamatter? You wanted an involved dad and that's what you're getting!*

Here's what's going through your wife's mind: *I've put out a million fires all day. I'm totally stressed out. And now Dad wants to play! And after winding him up, you expect him to conk out in ten minutes?*

Settle your kid down before bedtime or you'll undo your wife's hard work.

114. Read books to your baby.

It starts with those innocuous black-and-white board books. But soon you're on to *Pat the Bunny* and *Kiss the Boo-Boo* and *Goodnight Moon* and *Caps for Sale* and *Where the Wild Things Are* . . . and by the time you're reading *Green Eggs and Ham,* it'll be anybody's guess who's having more fun: you or your child.

At first, your baby is not likely to hold still while you're reading. Don't give up. There's something wonderful about that sweet little warm package cuddled up next to you in the feet pajamas, who's smacking the book or chewing on your forearm while you point to the pictures. One day, these readings will be one of your favorite times of the day. (You will, however, learn to edit unnecessary sentences out of your kid's book as you read—or you'll go totally nuts.)

BRING YOUR BABY TO THE CHILDREN'S SECTION OF THE BOOKSTORE. Thankfully, kids are now as welcome in bookstores as cappuccino. You can tell because the children's section of a bookstore looks as if a cyclone ripped half the books off the shelves and onto the floor. Keep an eye on your kid, have a ball, but know it's your job to show the common courtesy of cleaning up afterward.

---

115. Help your wife through Shoe Shock.

She'll be standing before her open closet, her fingers trembling, tears welling in her eyes. You wonder why, and here's the reason: for nine months before the baby was born, she realized her *life* would never be the same, but she hadn't considered her *feet* would never be. Some women's shoe sizes increase by a half size or more after pregnancy. And that means the end of her shoes as she's known them. Her shoes pinch. Her pinkie and big toe ache. She's getting blisters. Like a trooper humping through the hills, she'll take off her shoes and try to stretch them. Anything to keep her shoes! She's having *her* meltdown.

I found my wife standing before the neatly ordered pairs on the floor of her closet, knowing they'd never be on her feet again. "I got this pair before we were married," she was mumbling. "And I wore these the day you bought me our engagement ring. These on our honeymoon . . . " On and on.

So, what can you do? First admit to yourself (but not to her) that with your financial worries for the future, you weren't planning to buy her a new shoe collection. Admit also that if you're like most guys, you really can't comprehend your wife's love for shoes. You know it has something to do with sex—but you're not sure what (enclosure? tight fit? power in the heel? longer legs? youth?). Well, now is not the time to become the Plato of the Shoe Quandary! Realize this: When women meet, they go from eye contact to shoe contact. It's like a secret language guys don't speak (we'd never assess another living creature by his or her shoes).

Go with your wife and help her buy *one* new pair—all right, two pairs. Remind her to keep her former shoe collection for a year or so, just to be sure her feet don't mysteriously shrink again. (They probably won't.) Much later, she'll give her shoes to relatives and her closest friends, or to charity, or to your mother or your sisters—which will bond these women inextricably for life. (You don't have to understand.)

116. Accept your wife's gift of the extra-large sweater she wore during pregnancy (which now fits her like a burlap sack).

If your wife is anything like mine, there are some things she doesn't want to give to a pregnant girlfriend because they're emblems of *her* pregnancy. Remember how you felt when your then-girlfriend, now-wife wore your baggy button-down shirt (with nothing underneath) to make coffee in the morning? This is the reverse. So thrill her by wearing it—even if it's purple (like the one my wife gave me) and you feel like a sportscaster on the evening news whenever you have it on.

117. Don't be fooled by the False First Smile.

"Hurry quick!" I yelled to my wife when our baby flashed me a slobbery, sideways grin. It was magic and I didn't want my wife to miss it.

I lifted my daughter from her crib. Now her smile was even more effervescent and she waved her arms and legs wildly. "Ohh . . . ," my wife said. Suddenly, there was the startlingly loud sound of a balloon emptying: *pppbbfffffffttttt.* The smile faded as the resulting stench filled the room. My wife and I looked at one another, shrugged, and broke into laughter.

Oh, well, so we were amateurs—we'd wait for the real smile.

118. Enjoy your baby's first* real *smile.

A smile? At me? You'll feel as giddy as you did on your first high school date.

Fathers don't get much feedback—until now. When your baby beams at you, it's all worth it: the diapers, the sleeplessness, the times you were dog tired.

From this moment on, your connection to your baby is changed. Whenever you peer into the crib: a smile. Whenever you call out to your baby: a smile. You're connected!

119. Your baby's tears will break your heart.

Tears make it all real. They're so tiny, so fragile, and they collect at the corner of her eyes and trickle down her cheeks and collect where her neck sort of meets her shoulders. Until now, her cries were less real. Now they're snotty, sniffling affairs that end with you wishing you could just bring out your handkerchief and make it all go away.

120. Play peekaboo.

Your baby loves it and can chortle endlessly as you cover your face, hide, open and close your hands, spouting like an idiot, "Where's Daddy? Oh . . . here I am? Where's Daddy? Oh . . . I guess I'm here." This innocuous ploy informs your baby that you can go away and return; he finds it reassuring, if not entirely comprehensible.

121. Bring your baby to the movies with you.

Okay, let's make this perfectly clear: We're going to bend a rule, but nobody will get hurt.

Infants aren't welcome in movie theaters. Tough; society ought to get with it: New parents need a movie and often don't have a sitter.

Here's what you do: Put your baby in a front-style pack and zip up your coat (harder to sneak baby in if it's not winter). Stand in back. Your wife sits nearby. Open your coat so your baby doesn't overheat. Move from foot to foot to keep your baby asleep. When she awakens, bottle-feed (or your wife can breast-feed in total darkness). Stay as far from anyone as possible (which means, don't go to a popular movie on opening night).

Keep in motion so your baby stays calm. If she cries (and won't stop), exit the theater as quickly as possible, apologizing quietly (don't bother asking for a refund). But if you jostle around enough, you might keep her entertained for two hours—and it's great for your legs, arms, and love handles.

Show me a politician whose platform is "Infants to the Theaters!" and he's got my vote.

122. Set up a regular Daddy/Baby excursion.

The secret is regularity. Now's the time to pick a day and a time, then stick with it.

Remember that your baby won't get easily bored. Go to a park, then visit the Dalmatian at the fire station. Walk to a pond and skip stones. If it's afternoon, get a snack, then Rollerblade in the park. Go to the children's section of a bookstore. Visit an elderly relative or friend—but be sure to have time alone with your baby.

123. Be very cautious when strolling your baby across the street.

Lunatic drivers will cut within a millimeter of your stroller just to get to the next light. Yes, you can yell (as I often do), "The sign reads 'Walk!' " But that will only piss off the driver and won't prevent a catastrophe.

One technique I've discovered is to walk beside the stroller so your pushing arm is behind you. If you want to really get a driver's attention, wave a backpack at the same time. Yes, you'll look like Paul Revere riding through Boston swinging his lantern (or like a fool). But if you live in an urban area (or near a highway), your precaution is quite sane.

STABILIZE YOUR BABY'S STROLLER. Attach five-pound ankle or wrist weights (the type that closes with Velcro strips) to the area just above the stroller's front wheels. With no counterweight, here's what happens: You or your wife removes your baby from the stroller and the bag of groceries on the handle causes the stroller to crash to the ground and a few bottles to break and your baby to cry and you to point your finger and your wife to huff, "Get with the program!" (and you to sleep on the living room couch).

Yet another example of the relationship between Little Baby Stuff and Bedtime Stuff . . .

---

124. Know that women will perceive you as a father.

I took to the street with our two-month-old baby in a front-style pack. At the first street corner, a tall blonde with gazelle legs moved toward us. "Cute!! Cute!!"

She looked liked she had leapt off the pages of a fashion ad: chiseled features, the works. Plainly stated, I had never before even been a blip on the retina of a woman who looked like her. But while she gushed on about how adorable she thought little babies were, I considered how superficial her world seemed . . . and how much distance I felt from the single life. I sensed that she saw me as a Father, which was some sort of variant of a Man. Sure, a wedding band draws a line between you and single women—but not the way a baby does.

I felt liberated saying to her, "See you later. I'm taking my son to the park."

125. Talk to your baby on the phone.

Your wife might think you're nuts, but she can hold the receiver up to your baby's ear and you can yack away. Unfortunately, you'll soon hear a sound like a boat submerging into water: That's the mouthpiece going into your baby's mouth, which makes you want to laugh and cry.

TELL YOUR WIFE AND BABY YOU LOVE THEM. Often. As in: every day.

---

126. Bring your baby to work with you.

You can melt your coworkers' hearts. Everyone appreciates a baby, and you'll find the most ball-breaking workaholics on their hands and knees, smiling and gawking and making goo-goo, gaa-gaa noises. I'm not saying you should use your baby as a political tool to break down barriers, but I will say you'll temporarily roll back all bad office relations, giving you a chance to start anew with your coworkers.

127. You're going to be paranoid the first few times you leave your baby with a sitter.

It's ugly. You close the door, your baby is screaming her head off, you lean against the wall, your wife is sniffling, and you both walk slowly away. Then you stop. You tiptoe back to the door. You signal to your wife, *Shhh!* "What is it?" she mouths back. Maybe you say it, maybe you don't, but here's what's going through your head: *What if this woman is part of a kidnapping ring? She could hightail it to the airport to sell our baby in Latin America!* Maybe you show your true paranoia by going back inside, thereby inciting another bout of crying.

Hope your wife doesn't openly join in on your paranoia, or you're really in trouble. She has her paranoia, too—the sitter will drop your baby on his head, or let him fall, or cut himself, or . . . you get the idea. She says, "I'm just going to call home . . . make sure everything's all right," as soon as you enter the theater lobby. Or you catch her checking her watch, hoping the movie will end so she can make sure the baby is still okay.

You try not to show your haste as you both dash for your front door. But then: The baby is asleep, the sitter is folding clothes, sterilizing bottles, and emptying the trash . . . and you sigh and pretend you were never worried.

Take proper precautions ahead of time. Check out your sitter's references. Post emergency numbers. Carry a beeper. Get a cell phone. Then, enjoy your date.

128. So what do you look for in a baby-sitter?

Smarts help. Patience is important (teachers are great—they're used to twenty out-of-control kids, so what's one out-of-control kid?). So is reliability. (You will *not* be entertained when you miss a concert or a business dinner because your baby-sitter didn't show up.) Housecleaning ability helps. (If your baby sleeps, you don't want to pay for someone to watch TV.) Sweetness is important. Consistency. Protectiveness. But most important is the ability to care.

Our longtime baby-sitter was possibly the least prompt person in the surrounding five counties. (She once showed up at seven P.M. when we were expecting her at noon, shrugged, and said, "Is something wrong?") Our friends all said, "How do you spell *fired*?" But she was the Mary Poppins of baby handlers: The instant she came, our babies were calm, smiley, contented.

We bought her a watch, and eight years later, she's like a part of our family.

129. Help your wife conquer baby-sitter envy.

Your wife will be upset the day your baby seems madly in love with the nanny or baby-sitter. Look out if your baby throws a fit and your wife can't calm her but the baby-sitter can. My friend Gina, who works at home one day a week, said, "Our nanny has everything under control. I sometimes cringe when I hear giggles and good times from downstairs. The other day, my son started crying hysterically and the nanny couldn't settle him. I went whistling down the stairs because my son was crying!"

Logic fails here. "But you *want* him to like the sitter" won't work on your wife. Just help her understand that no matter what, she'll always be number one with the baby.

130. Never admit that a baby-sitter is attractive.

Sooner or later, your baby will get a baby-sitter that will make you wish *you* were the baby and could stay home instead of going out. Your wife knows that this twenty-year-old beauty, lying in her perfectly fitting jeans on your couch with your baby, looks like the mommies in all the TV commercials. This doesn't make your wife entirely happy and that prompts her to ask if you noticed. Your answer is (or better be) no.

We've had our share of attractive baby-sitters, but one in particular raised a stir. Friends would practically get whiplash from their heads snapping as she walked by. Invariably, someone would wait until she was out of earshot to ask my wife, "Don't you mind having her in the house?" To which my wife would shrug her shoulders and say, "I don't mind if he looks at her. Of course if he touched her, I'd kill him." (Our terms were pretty straightforward.)

Let your wife make all arrangements with baby-sitters. It's awkward when you telephone a baby-sitter at her home: You get her groggy-voiced roommate (at eleven A.M.!) or her parents, who ask who's calling, and despite every rational cell in your brain, you feel . . . awkward. Your wife might resent your lack of involvement in baby-sitter arrangements, so make it up elsewhere.

131. There's no such thing as a cheap date anymore.

You quickly discover that a movie date for the two of you is no longer a minor proposition (particularly in a big city). Eighteen bucks (tickets), plus forty bucks (sitter), plus ten bucks (taxi/parking), plus ten bucks (two glasses of mediocre Chardonnay at a bistro to help you cope with the awfulness of leaving your screaming baby), plus ten more bucks (two more glasses of mediocre Chardonnay to help you cope with the awfulness of the movie), plus fifteen bucks (the sitter's taxi home, since the discussion of the trauma of leaving made it too late for the sitter to take a bus or the subway.) That's over a hundred bucks to see a movie so bad you wanted to leave after the opening credits!

Of course you can always rent a two-dollar video, uncork a bottle of wine, and put the savings toward your kid's college education.

---

5 TIPS ON DATING YOUR WIFE:

1. Start early—around six-thirty. An eight o'clock date means you're too wiped out to enjoy yourselves.
2. Explore. Don't just go to movies and the same old eating or drinking haunts. Part of what made dating great was you saw new things. Don't stop now.
3. Tune out of Father mode. Your wife isn't interested in a date with Ward Cleaver. Flick a switch and turn into the dude who knew how to capture a woman's heart.
4. Don't moan, "I'm so wiped out . . . I'm so wiped out." Your wife wants to feel young—and doesn't. She's depending on you to keep things spicy.

5. Find a private spot that spells romance for you and your wife: a bridge, a view, a café where you watch the world walk by. You both need it.

132. Buy an airplane ticket and go (with your new family).

Contrary to the cliché of the infant screaming over the roar of a jet engine, many newborns are terrific travelers. Call the airlines and ask about restrictions. If your baby is less than three weeks old, you'll probably need a doctor's note to board the plane. Most airlines don't charge extra if you or your wife holds your infant throughout the flight. (There's usually a 50 percent ticket discount for a baby in a car seat.)

The first six months are the optimal travel time. (After that, it gets considerably tougher.) If you've got frequent flier miles, use them, or find a special low fare—they exist. I saved up vacation time so we could take our month-old daughter away. My wife nursed while we taxied on the runway; then our baby slept for an entire seven-hour flight. My friends Hamilton and Laura brought their infant to Ireland and toasted their good fortune in a tiny pub, a liter of beer in one hand, a baby in the other. (Be sure to get a passport for your baby if you go to another country.)

The biggest surprise of travels with your baby is the special treatment you'll get from strangers. It's thrilling to hear compliments about your adventurousness; it makes you and your wife feel, well, extraordinary.

133. Pack essentials in a carry-on bag.

Airlines can—and do—lose luggage. Diapers, formula, drops for ear pressure, a first aid kit, and essential toilet articles belong with other can't-lose-'em things in a carry-on bag.

Otherwise, you and your wife may end up shouting at each other while your baby wails because she needs a new diaper (and all the stores are closed for Christmas break and won't be open until you, your wife, and your baby have all lost it big time).

Another tip: Pack an empty, lightweight duffel bag on the bottom of a suitcase. Invariably, you'll buy things that you forgot to pack (like sand buckets and shovels), which you won't want to throw away on the last day. We brought a duffel on every trip and it never went back empty.

10 THINGS YOU SHOULD KNOW BEFORE YOU TRAVEL:

1. You have to leave home early enough, in case everything goes wrong en route to your plane, that you'll still have time to make it.
2. You'll feel like a hired mule as you lug your family's many bags to the check-in.
3. You'll feel like a hired mule as you haul all your carry-on items on the plane.

4. If you're going to another country, you will never think of bringing enough disposable diapers along (and you'll wonder how parents there get by on their country's inferior diapers).
5. If you have an older child, he will dash off into a crowd at the airport.
6. None of your baby's favorite rattles, kiddie books, coloring books, puzzles, and snacks will seem appealing on the plane. He would rather pull down the seat tray five thousand times.
7. If your baby sleeps, the other passengers will think you're perfect parents. If your baby cries, they will be tempted to ask a flight attendant if the three of you could be jettisoned from the plane with parachutes.
8. Don't bother bringing a book or newspaper for yourself because you'll never have a chance to read it.
9. Know you'll need a vacation before your vacation and a vacation after your vacation to rest from your vacation.

134. Don't let anyone call you "Mr. Mom."

The term sucks. It implies that you're trying to imitate a mother. You're not. Fatherhood is totally different than motherhood. We rough-and-tumble, shoulder the weight, give our baby something to lean on, take her out into the world, teach her to walk, swing, and fly, and help her to stand up for who she is and what she is, and not to budge.

Stand against a wall. Feel the support. Take a step away. The wall represents you—a father—which has nothing to do with motherhood's enveloping quality.

135. Get ready for Pacifier Madness.

This tiny bit of nipple-shaped plastic is sure to arouse more genuine hostility per square centimeter than anything you've known before or since. Don't be deceived by the cutesy nicknames (binkie, mimi). This pacifier might pacify your baby, but not everybody else. Almost immediately, everyone will ask, "Aren't you worried about getting her off it?" Or "Don't you think you're using the 'binkie' just a bit too often?"

No! Your peace of mind is worth every corruptive instant that the pacifier is employed. Tell all those busybodies that this is not a narcotic, this is plastic—the defining medium of our age.

How easily we get hooked on things plastic. Yank it out and your baby looks like an irate Winston Churchill minus his stogie. Leave it in and your baby puffs on that thing in a rather disturbing manner: eyes fixed ahead, cheeks pulling in, swelling out.

It probably *will* be hard to get your baby off it, but not impossible. Our daughter simply lost interest one day. But not our son. So we intentionally "lost" all his pacifiers and explained the sad situation to him. (Needless to say, he didn't like our absentmindedness.) But after one or two days of fits, he forgot about them—and we saw his lips again for the first time in months. One friend said he and his wife limited pacifiers to when their baby was in her crib, which made it far easier for her to stop. Another dipped the pacifiers into vinegar (to create a bitter taste). Yet another cut the nipple portion in half so it was less satisfying. (Yes, these remedies sound cruel, but sometimes they're necessary.)

For now, let baby have his day. And buy a dozen of exactly the same kind. There's nothing less pacifying than no pacifier when baby expects one.

136. You might miss your wife's pregnancy madness.

One friend told me his wife wasn't sure if she wanted a Taurus or a Gemini for their second child, and since it was nearly ten P.M. on the night of horoscope transition, she actually said to him, "Quick, run down to the hospital gift shop. Buy *Bazaar* or *Mademoiselle,* bring them up here, and read the horoscopes for the two signs." While he dashed down the stairs, she asked the nurse to slow down the Pitocin (the drug her doctor was using to speed up labor). Back in the labor room, huffing wildly, he read the outlooks for Taurus and Gemini. She considered for a moment, then said, "You know, I think two iron-willed/soft interiors in one family is too much. I'll go with a Taurus. Get me back on Pitocin." And she got her Taurus.

Early parenthood just isn't that wild—unless you make it that way. Come home with take-out Chinese, throw down a picnic cloth, and let your baby lie on her back and watch you eat with chopsticks. Feed each other. Dress your baby and mock-dance her across a counter to "Love Shack." Do all the stuff you used to do *before* you had a baby. Don't lose your spontaneity or your marriage will suffer.

137. Don't rush to celebrate when your baby sleeps through the night.

You'll swear it's the finest night you've ever had. It was so simple: You hit the hay and woke up after sunrise. You'll stretch, smile, and want to tell the world. Don't—or the Gods of Sleep will turn the tables on your baby and you will receive a score of sleepless nights for your bragging.

But don't let it go unnoticed. Have a cup of coffee in bed with your wife before she serves breakfast to your baby.

138. Celebrate six months.

Bring home flowers and a bottle of bubbly (or a cupcake with six tiny candles, which will make your wife say, "Ohh . . . "). Make a fuss, because you and your wife deserve a ton of credit. Can you believe how long it took you to change your first diaper? Or that you'd never burped a baby? Take a moment to feel good about your accomplishment and how much you've got to look forward to with your baby.

3.

CRAWLING DAYS:
Six to Twelve Months

139. Batten down the hatches! Plug the sockets! Get everything extraneous off the floor! Your baby is crawling!

You've looked forward to this in much the way you did the delivery day—with little comprehension of the changes it brings about. Your baby might begin to crawl at six or seven or eight months old, but don't get bent out of shape if your baby is a late crawler (do call the pediatrician to discuss your worry). For days now, your baby has been crawling backward, like a seal confronted with a polar bear. Now, he's ready to zip across the floor in forward motion. You smile. It's magic. Maybe there's a lump in your throat—that's all right!

But before you can kick back on the couch to watch the show, your baby scoots for the stairs! Or the glass-shelved bookcase! Or your wife's purse, spilling with lipstick and mirrors and a bottle of aspirin! Or your briefcase with pages that simply cannot be scattered! Time to readjust your thinking—and your living quarters, which seemed like a pretty safe place until today. Now, every stairwell looks like it was designed by Hitchcock; every medicine, kitchen, laundry room, or workroom cabinet contains enough toxins to kill a platoon; and every electrical socket carries more voltage than an electric chair. Welcome to the danger zone you call home.

Good news: You can learn to safeguard all these places. You'll place plastic plugs in sockets, locks over cabinets and oven and stove knobs, gates over stairways, and all the rest. But understand you'll never create a *totally* safe haven for your baby.

140. Expect the unexpected.

Our little boy once picked up a water spray bottle, squirted a light switch, and then screamed in terror as flames shot out a foot from the wall. Every dad can recount his horror stories: the time his baby grabbed a plastic bag to wear as a hat or chewed on glass or discovered where Daddy keeps his darts. Moral? Someday you may need to know emergency medical procedures, so take a Baby Life course (and later, consider a refresher course).

141. Keep a baby CPR book near your medicine cabinet.

Memorize the procedures. Test your babysitter or nanny—and if she needs a refresher Baby Life course, pay and ask her to go. Everyone in your home should feel confident in case of an emergency.

142. Get a first aid kit.

They range in price from ten to seventy bucks at an outdoors store or drugstore. Or, if you're tight on cash, copy down the item list from the back of a good kit and create your own. Be sure to include a special tick-removing tweezers, with a little magnifying glass built in. (And if you live in a tick-infested area, check your child daily.)

143. Buy ice packs and store them in your freezer.

When your kid is howling because he's banged himself up, an ice pack may be the only thing that calms him. (Ice cubes wrapped in a towel or placed in a baggy work well, also.)

144. Post emergency numbers near your phones.

The list should include the phone number and address of the pediatrician, the emergency room, an ambulance service (from your preferred hospital), your work, your wife's work, relatives or friends who could offer assistance, and the pharmacy. You should also have the numbers of you and your wife's cell phone and beeper, the police and fire departments, and the national poison control center. Write in red your child's allergies or medical conditions.

145. Don't turn your home into a giant baby room.

I had some friends who gave their home over to their baby's stuff. Nothing would have prepared me for the sight. All the furniture was pushed to the room's perimeter and baby toys were *everywhere.* You couldn't walk without something squeaking or triggering a Barney "heh-heh-heh" or a "hickory-dickory-dock."

Don't give in or you'll feel like a trespasser in your own home. Rotate your baby's toys to storage and back to retain his interest (and your aesthetic sanity). Buy wicker baskets for quick storage. Install shelves in closets for toys and games. Get a dresser for the baby's clothes. Later, you'll teach your child to clean up after herself, but for now, it's your job.

146. Help your wife store infant stuff.

It happens fast. By six or seven months, you've got a pile of stuff your baby no longer needs: a carriage, a bassinet, maybe a small crib, piles of too-small clothes. The stuff looks like it belonged to a doll.

It's up to you to help stash these things away, or you'll be living in a museum of early babyhood. No, don't give all of it away just yet (you might have other babies). The serious sifting won't happen for a while because your wife won't part with any but the most spit-on soiled items.

Later, give early baby stuff to friends or find a charity and donate stuff you'll never use again. If you keep everything endlessly, there might be, one day, a payoff. My parents kept virtually everything of mine (and my siblings') until their basement was piled nearly to the ceiling. We all laughed about it, until my kids discovered the treasure trove. Now, when they visit Grandma and Grandpa, they head straight for the deep recesses of the basement to romp on the ancient rocking horse, to turn on the player piano, and to rummage through games and books that no longer exist in today's world.

147. Pet alert!

Once your baby crawls, the stakes have risen considerably in the tenuous relationship with your pet (who likely feels ousted from his perch as King of the Castle) and your baby (who is the challenger). Once he learned to crawl, my friends Marina and Caleb's boy went directly to their dog Mutley's sleeping pillow—not a great idea, because of the dog's predilection for humping his pillow. "We had to teach Mutley it was okay to hump his pillow (we wash it once a week) but *not* okay to try to hump our new crawler," said Marina. "Then we had to teach our baby that it wasn't okay to hog Mutley's pillow."

The troubles with pets aren't confined to dogs. Just after bringing home their baby, my friends Raoul and Trish's cat "became neurotic and started crapping incessantly at the front door—which is a cat's way of saying *trouble.*" A friend suggested a pet shrink, who came over to their house and played soothing New Age music to the unreceptive ears of the cat. The cat hid beneath the couch while its owners, who hate New Age music, rolled their eyes. "We learned not to punish the cat and not to lock her out of the baby's room, so it wasn't a total waste," Raoul concluded.

DON'T START RUNNING A DISASTER MOVIE IN YOUR HEAD. Any number of things could go wrong with your family, and your mind goes crazy with the prospects. If you took each one seriously, you'd go nuts. Just get on with being a dad. If millions of guys can deal with all these what-ifs, so can you.

---

148. Keep your chemistry in check.

For me, that means at least a twenty-minute workout each day. Those little endorphins are my good buddies; they keep me from getting too whacked out.

No time, you say? In fatherhood, I've found three times to exercise: before the baby wakes up, during my lunch hour, or after he goes to sleep. Try a late-night jump rope—a great way to flush out the day's woes.

149. Know that weekends won't always be relaxing.

Many of my buddies admitted they couldn't wait to scramble back to work on Monday morning after a weekend from hell.

If you feel that, keep it to yourself. Your wife may be wiped out, too, but she's not in the mood for your male incomprehension. Women, in general, are more able to say, "Hey, it's the price you pay for having this beautiful creature."

Although many mothers dream of the three of you navigating an entire weekend together (minute by minute and second by second), I think alternating time with the baby can be a sanity saver: (the old Divide and Conquer mentality . . .). After a week of work, men need some downtime—alone.

When you are together, seek out places that promote good old family fun. Go to a park with a blanket and a picnic. Place your baby on the blanket, then, with your wife holding one set of corners and you holding the others, lift your baby and watch glee spread over his face. Play airplane. All this stuff makes your weekend special.

150. Learn the difference between structure and discipline.

Structure is setting boundaries so your kid has limits. Discipline is, well, a lot more complex because it involves punishment and obedience. Many of us grew up in homes where Dad was the Disciplinarian, the end of the line of bad behavior. He was the guy with the belt or bar of soap in his hand. In today's world of the involved father, discipline has become a dirty word.

Try not to think of it that way. You've got to teach your child rules. Later, you'll have to learn about "time outs" and all sorts of tough parenting stuff. For now, you and your wife ought to get your signals straight. Discuss your views on discipline and your fears about it. I told my wife I never wanted her to say, "Just wait until your father hears about this!" We both agreed that we don't believe in spanking or pulling a kid by his ear or washing his mouth out with soap. But until I learned, "No means no," I was letting my kid down.

You have two goals with regularity, structure, and discipline: unity between you and your wife, and your baby's self-esteem.

151. Keep a private sanctuary.

Every guy needs a room or a space of his own—an office, den, woodworking shop, workout room, or attic hideout—where everything is his own. For me, that's my writing studio, where I know things are as I leave them, and nobody's going to affix a peanut butter and jelly sandwich to my computer screen. Without your own space, you'll get testy and irritable.

152. Alter your diet so you have more energy.

Shortly after our baby was born, I realized I needed more energy to get by on less sleep, less downtime. One buddy suggested his own variation of the U.S. Ski Team diet: steak, grapefruit, and tomatoes. While I'd always wanted to look like Robert Redford in *Downhill Racer,* I thought, *Better get another opinion.*

"Cut bagels from your diet," another friend said. Yet another: "Eat ninety percent of your diet by five o'clock and you'll sleep more soundly." At my local health food store, one customer told me, "You really ought to try drinking only carrot juice." I noticed the man's skin was Halloween orange. "*Only* carrot juice?" I said, thinking, *I bet it's easy for your wife to find you in the dark.*

Finally, the store's Bangladeshi chef introduced me to a brown rice and vegetable mush that he prepared with spring water, no oils, no fats, no salt, and delicious spices. He offered me a glass of mixed vegetable juice to chase the rice and vegetables. The dish is sufficiently pungent to turn heads when I bring it on an airplane (my wife shrugs to other passengers, "I don't know him"), but tastes good enough to eat every day and gives me the oomph I need for fatherhood.

153. Prepare your home for a standing baby.

Long before she can walk, your baby will yank herself up on her feet while she holds a bookcase or coffee-table top. Now's the time for you to clear off tabletops of anything that you don't want her grasping hold of or knocking down. Draw an imaginary line around your room at about hip height, then remove anything that might hurt the baby or might get damaged.

From this perch, your baby will see the world anew. She can see out windows and into other rooms, over chair tops and into drawers. The world is opening up.

Suddenly, she topples. Here's your chance to be a real dad—that is, her support. Encourage her, ease her up to her perch again.

154. Get used to distractions.

Before you had a baby, you might have needed total quiet when you worked at home. Well, that's often no longer possible. Now, you'll have to learn to make calls or pay bills with your kids dangling off your arms and legs or throwing balls across the room.

Leave a room before you lose it, which will only alienate you from your wife. Learn to say, "Hold on, I'm taking this call on another phone," or "Honey, if you take the baby out for half an hour, I'll do the same afterward." Try to focus more, but know your limits.

155. Play the pointing game.

When your baby is about nine months old, he'll begin pointing at random objects and looking into your eyes for an explanation. You'll start with face parts: "Eyes!" or "Mouth!" (It can go on all day.) Soon, he'll be on to "Bird!" Or "Tree!" What keeps you going is your baby's excited eyes, his lopsided smile, the drool on his chin. He's having a ball—and, admit it, so are you. (Could you possibly have imagined you'd be enjoying this?)

Don't be a drag and try to read the paper while your baby wants you to play. Here's a chance for you to engage your baby until one of you is ready to collapse.

156. Get a box with lots of hinges.

When your baby is about ten months old, she'll have a hinge fetish. At a video store, she'll yank videos off the shelf and play with the covers while the videos crash down. She'll flutter the covers of books or open and close doors or anything else with a hinged movement. You can get irritated as you stand amid total mess, or you can get creative.

If you're handy, construct a wooden box with lots of hinged openings. Or, if you're like me, buy one at the toy store.

157. Your baby is not the most detrimental thing that has ever happened to your sex life.

Let's keep it in perspective: Losing your job or leaving your briefcase and wallet in a taxi or being overinvested when the stock market melts will kill your sex life quicker than any colicky baby will. When you see a young, hot couple, don't say to your wife, "He's going to get laid." She'll tell you, "That's such a *guy* thing to say," and she'll fret that you're sulking about your sex life and making noises as if you'd like to be in that guy's shoes (or, more precisely, his girlfriend's bed).

158. Don't romanticize past girlfriends. Romanticize your wife.

After months of endless talk of ear infections and vacillations in your baby's digestive tract, there's an alarming tendency for a guy to romanticize the steamy days of past girlfriends. And why not? Your life now is more regimented than the average inmate's at Sing Sing—and you're considerably less rested than the dude in the blue work jumper, too.

Sure, you remember one girlfriend in particular (for me, it was my Italian flame and her favorite phrase that stuck in my mind: "There are two things in life: coffee and love, in that order"). But the past is no place to hang out—not when right over there your wife is quietly breast-feeding your baby in a corner of the couch. When she looks up at you and smiles, you need to remember why you wanted, finally, to trade freedom for commitment.

159. Know that your wife may be disappointed if she doesn't lose her pregnancy weight quickly.

Every pregnant woman secretly (and irrationally) believes she'll balloon up, pop out the baby, then shrink back down.

Sorry, but it often doesn't work out that way. Those added pounds may hang on and on. Be oblivious to it. Gently bend the truth until she gets her weight back down—which she will, eventually.

160. Listen to your wife's fantasies—then act on them.

Sometimes it's as simple as having your wife far enough from the baby for her to feel closer to her wild side. One female friend, whose husband is an administrator at a prep school, said it turned her on to think about having sex on the couch in his office at night with all the students tucked away in their rooms. (See, women can think in *Penthouse Forum*–ese, too.)

161. Don't worry—you're not the first couple to slow down having sex in the first six months.

Unfortunately, you can't pick up a magazine without seeing an article written by a married couple that professes to have sex every day for a month straight. (Sure . . .) But nobody's told you the simple truth: You'll have less sex in the beginning of parenthood because it's the price you pay for having a baby.

There will be awkward moments. My wife and I were traveling with our five-month-old baby. It was ten o'clock and all was well. We were reading and our baby was sleeping, when we heard a couple moaning and having wild sex in the hotel room next to ours. Their headboard started to pound so hard against our wall that I thought the couple would crash through. I said to my wife, "I can't even read. My book is jiggling." Finally, I suggested we take our baby out for an evening stroll. We held hands. We smooched. And when we came back to our room: quiet. Both of us knew our sex life would return to normal, but we didn't need a noisy reminder of what we weren't doing just yet.

PREPARE TO HEAR THESE WORDS: "OHHH . . . JUST PUT IT IN AND THEN I CAN GO TO SLEEP."

---

162. Treat your wife as you would a mistress.

Loving. Playfully. Adventurously. Flirtingly.

163. Other men could be flirting with your wife.

The temptation is to think, "No guy will cast a glance at a new mother." Uh-huh. Six months after she had delivered our baby, my wife was walking down Broadway when a young, single man said, "Excuse me, can I bother you for a moment?" She paused. "I just wanted to compliment you on your legs," the man continued. "You've got beautiful legs and I wanted you to know."

Right then, you want your wife to whip the Mace from her purse, spray it in this dude's eyes, stomp his feet, knee him in the groin, and whistle for the nearest cop to throw him in the slammer for the rest of his days. So what does she say? "That's very sweet of you. You've made my day." (When he asks her out for coffee, she says, "Thanks, anyway," and walks away.)

The point is, a new dad has a tendency to think his up-to-her-neck-in-diapers wife is off the market. Bad idea. Just when you least expect it, some other guy could be hitting on her. It's a chilling reminder that you can never stop romancing your woman.

164. Be amused when the food goes everywhere (but into your baby's mouth).

You pretend the baby's spoon filled with baby-food peas is really an airplane hoping to come in for a landing in your baby's mouth. *Bzzzzzz-zzzzz. Captain to Ground Control, Captain to Ground Control. Do we have clearance to land? Repeat: Do we have clearance to land?* Your baby smiles, the mouth opens, and you zoom toward your destination. When: *whack!* The baby's arm smacks the plane out of your hands. Now the gunk's all over your face and the wall and the floor and the ceiling and the phone and the TV—everywhere but in your baby's mouth.

A recipe for going berserk, right? Only if you insist on seeing it that way. Babies are not neat, tidy eaters, so learn to keep your cool amidst the mess. Once, when it looked like a vat of prune purée had exploded in our kitchen, my three-year-old daughter shrugged and said, "I think he wants baby-food pizza." Now *there's* an idea.

165. Prepare your car for the baby.

For the next few years, it will be a toss-up as to who hates the car more: you or your baby. Consider the baby's perspective: the two power people take the controls, Captain and Disc Jockey, while poor, dumb, stupid, stuck-in-a-car-seat baby sits in back, looking at the back of the glory couple's heads, hearing smidgens of conversation and Raffi played too low to enjoy. *It just ain't right.*

So time your trips. We would sometimes wait until our baby's eyelids were blue with exhaustion, get her into her baby seat, rev the engine, and know she'd be out by the next light. My wife and I would then pretend we were scooting off on an adventure and catch up on the day's events. Later, when our kids were past the napping stage, we stocked the backseats with a tape recorder per kid, earphones, plenty of tapes, extra batteries, books, and pillows—which works at least sometimes.

BRING A CHANGE OF YOUR BABY'S CLOTHES FOR CAR TRIPS.

---

166. It will be tougher getting out the door.

It takes about twenty minutes to collect everything, forget something, go back, and finally close the door. "We've missed church four weeks in a row," one friend said. "It was just one thing or another, and we finally gave up."

Help your wife with organization. Know what goes in the diaper bag: two bottles, a cup, diapers, wipes, toys, snacks, books, a burpee cloth—whatever. It helps to write a list of what you ought to pack; that way, your wife doesn't have to remind you and you don't feel inept.

167. Know how to dress your baby so you don't twist his fingers.

For now, he's going to be wearing T-shirts and jumpsuits, and everything everybody gave you as gifts. Stretch the neck really wide (your baby's head is huge in relation to everything else), and pull it over. Next, pull the sleeve open, push your hand in, and pull your baby's hand through—otherwise, you'll twist every finger on your baby's sure-to-be-the-next-great-concert-pianist's hand.

There will be moments when one arm pops out while you pull a leg through and vice versa, until you break out in a sweat. Try not to lose your cool.

168. Know how, when, and where to eat out with your baby.

In France, people eat out with their dogs, but babies are frowned upon. In Italy, chefs come out of kitchens in white aprons to greet babies. In America, we're somewhere in between.

Dine early, before the restaurant gets crowded, or stroll around and around the block, then go into the restaurant after your baby is securely asleep. Although most babies can snooze through just about anything, you'll feel more relaxed if you maximize the baby's chances of staying conked out through the entire meal.

Here's the ideal spot for your baby: tucked in a corner booth, standing on a plastic banquette to see a fish tank, with a jukebox nearby (with lots of swirling lights), friendly waiters, a kiddie menu, and fast service.

Since you won't always have these conditions, bring crayons, paper, books, a blanket—basically, a portable playroom so you can have a few moments to eat.

169. Public bathrooms present an awkward problem for you and your baby.

If you've got a boy, you probably don't mind too much having to bring him into a smelly room with men leaning over urinals while cigarette ashes fall on their potbellies.

But what do you do if you're out with your little girl and you've got to pee? Or she needs a change? Or, after she's potty trained, she needs to use the toilet? Sure, there are changing tables in some men's rooms (especially in airports and movie theaters), but they're not nearly as frequent as in women's rooms. If one's not to be found, you go into the men's room, hightail it to a stall, do your thing, then dash out. Or you steel yourself, knock on the women's room door, explain your situation if there's someone there, and ask if it is all right to bring your baby girl to the changing table (if you need to change a diaper) or into a stall (if she's toilet trained). Usually, women are so thrilled to see a daddy out with his little girl that they'll happily share the women's room with you.

170. Take baths with your baby.

Stay in until your fingertips shrivel. But never turn your back, even for an instant. That's all it takes for your baby to go underwater. Call your wife if you need help.

171. Don't believe in "no tears" shampoo.

172. You and your wife will miss your baby's early months.

You just want to freeze the moment so you can peer into it like a clear, fossilized rock. It's that same sensation you used to have as a kid at the end of summer: time slipping away.

Unfortunately, you can't. So try to stay focused on what's happening now, or it will pass right by.

173. Show your wife your future together.

She's not the first woman to worry that you'll leave her with the baby and her steaming diapers.

Words are fine, but actions speak louder. When our baby was seven months old, I dashed to a liquidation sale at a big sporting goods store, bought a pair of kiddie skis (Rossignols for ten dollars!) and six pairs of in-line skates (for less than the price of wheels!) to keep my kid blading until she was eight years old. My wife took one look at my bounty and threw her arms around me. Another time, when our daughter was still an infant, I bought a polka dot skirt she wouldn't wear until she was two. This was another major hit with my wife. Both times, it meant that I could *envision* our future—and it really touched the right chord.

PLANT A TREE IN HONOR OF YOUR CHILD'S BIRTH. Go to a nursery, select a tree, then ask your wife to help you pick the right spot in your yard. Because trees mark time not so much in years but in decades (and even generations), you and your wife will instantly begin envisioning yourselves lying in the shade of the tree with your teenager.

One tip: Choose a low-maintenance tree. Which means no apple trees, no matter how vividly you can envision your kid picking an apple from atop your shoulders.

---

174. For your baby's teething, you can always try whiskey.

My wife headed out to the pharmacy to buy gum-numbing cream but came home empty-handed—the store was closed. "Don't worry," I said. "We've got the active ingredient in that formula right here." I pulled out a bottle of bourbon, figuring that if this stuff was good enough to undo a grown man's woes, it might calm our baby's deep-lunged exclamations of pain.

I dabbed my finger in, then rubbed it on her upper gums. *Hummm.* She licked her lips and seemed to be deciding whether it was from Kentucky (yes), if it was properly aged (yes), and if the advertising campaign featured old geezers whose ancestors worked a still by the light of the moon (yes). A look came over her face that said, *I think I'll roll over and go to sleep now.* It worked.

For a short while. Our baby woke up a few hours later and a few hours after that. (Amazingly, we'd nearly forgotten just how tough no sleep is.) By morning, my wife and I, in dire need of a jolt, were dipping our baby's zwiebacks into our Starbucks while our baby teethed a bagel.

175. Prepare to be unnerved when your baby grinds her teeth.

(Think of a fingernail running over a chalkboard and you get the picture.)

176. Search for perspective from your child's illness.

The pediatrician says, "There's nothing to worry about, but . . . we want to do some blood work to rule out all possibilities." You stammer, "What possibilities?" But even while the doctor is assuring you that your baby's fever or bruised leg really is probably nothing more, you're envisioning the worst, culling from the recesses of your mind news stories about kids suffering from rare diseases, and you're promising yourself you'll stop worrying about the petty stuff *from now on.*

Good. Illness gives pause. We assess things anew. We see more clearly. We make resolutions, some of which we might even keep. Share with your wife your new clarity so she can help you make minor adjustments in your fatherly course.

177. Help your wife with important medical decisions.

It's awfully tough to see through the jungle of medical jargon when it comes time for a medical decision. That's why it's your job to make the necessary calls for second opinions and to sift through the data.

When our daughter was two and a half, her dentist took my wife aside and said all was not well. Then, he recounted a gruesome list of necessary procedures: eight cavities needed filling, four teeth needed capping, all needed coating with fluoride. "It's got to be done," he said in an ominous tone. "I know it's a lot of money. But you wouldn't want to fail your daughter." My wife nearly cried on the spot.

I returned with my wife the next day—I didn't believe the prognosis. I suggested we get second and third opinions from other qualified doctors, who said, "But these are baby teeth. If we closely monitor the cavities' progress, we can probably avoid any dental work, because the teeth will fall out naturally." Which is precisely what happened.

We kept our money and our sanity and our daughter avoided unnecessary procedures.

178. Keep a list of baby's words.

Every kid devises his own vocabulary. *Gunk-gunk!* was TV for the longest time for our daughter. *Sacki! Sacki!,* our son would cry whenever he saw a taxi whiz past. Your child will have equally charming (to you) jargon, but it'll be lethally dull for everyone else on the planet—especially to an older sibling, who will roll her eyes, sigh, and announce her assessment of her younger sibling's limited mental capacity to anyone who will listen.

You won't remember any but a few of your baby's code words unless you write them down in your journal.

179. Help your wife organize your kid's first birthday party.

Admit it: As milestones go, this is major. So get involved! You'll feel less an outsider if you help design the cake, draw up a list of baby cronies, and load the camera.

Don't go overboard. There's a disturbing tendency in some circles to bury the beauty of the day with an extravaganza. Better to invite your kid's very best playmates and some of your friends.

180. Temper your Early Riser.

A few tips: Don't feed your baby the instant she awakens; don't give her juice in her crib; do make her crib a mini–recreation room with enough nifty creature comforts so she can entertain herself. And be sure to have good window blinds so she doesn't awaken with the first light of dawn.

181. Don't feel weird when your wife falls in love with your baby's behind.
Instead, go to the gym and do some butt exercises so she casts a fleeting glance at your derriere occasionally, too.

YOUR BABY'S DEVELOPMENT ISN'T NEAT OR ORDERED. If you pay too close attention to The Books, you're liable to get pretty bent out of shape when everything doesn't go exactly as planned—and it never goes exactly as planned.

---

182. Don't be competitive with other babies.
You go to a playground and all the parents get a slightly paranoid look in their eyes. Someone will say, "Your baby is how old? And she's still crawling?!" Or "He's not walking yet?! Mine started months ago." Or "How many words does he speak?"

Call your baby's pediatrician if you have concerns. But realize that it all balances out in the end. We once watched a baby fill in the missing words to *Goodnight Moon.* I went sheet white, and my wife elbowed me. "Don't feel that way," she said—and she was right.

From then on, I tried to focus on what our children could do in relation to themselves, not others. It's much easier that way.

183. Carry your wife over the threshold.
Not long after the first birthday party, my wife got her rain check cashed from the day we brought the baby home. We were coming back from the

grocery store when I asked my wife to set down her bag of diapers, baby wipes, and baby food. I swept her off her feet, carried her across the threshold, kissed her.

I held her there for a moment and started to laugh until I thought I'd drop her. We both knew that in about two minutes we'd slip back into the tumult of parenthood. But for a moment, we'd managed to recapture a bit of that romanticism that started us on the whole enterprise in the first place.

4.

WALKING DAYS:
The Second Year

184. Hold out your hands and help your child walk.

This is a real daddy thing. One day, there'll be an I-can-do-it look in your baby's eyes. Everything is about to change. She's held onto countless tabletops and rails and bookshelves. Crawling is suddenly a bore. She's going to do it; you sense the urgency.

Hold her hands. Encourage her. Take steps backward. She takes clomping, big, Frankenstein-like steps, arms out, head back, knees high. It's a sight. Her knees buckle under and you catch her. But then, you sense a new strength; that's the moment to gently let her go.

And there she goes! Five, six, seven steps before she's down. But nothing will ever be the same. She's off, and it's only a day or two until she'll never crawl again. Grab your wife, grab your camera; hug one, snap the other. Let your joy show.

My daughter learned to walk on vacation in a hotel hallway, and the glee in her eye will forever remain fixed in my mind. I've got a photo of her, face flushed, exultant. The next day we hopped on a plane, and from the moment the seat belt sign came off, we were up and down the aisle. Other passengers sensed the novelty, smiled, patted her on the back, caught her when the plane rocked. Six hours later, I trudged off the plane, my back killing me—but ecstatic nonetheless.

NO, ITS NOT TOO LATE TO GET INVOLVED AS A FATHER. Some guys just aren't into the early phase of fathering. If that's how you felt, it doesn't mean you can't change. Think of Roger Clemens standing on the mound, spotting his paltry early-season numbers on the scoreboard (5–6, with an unwieldy ERA), taking a deep breath, and promising himself that from now on, he'd let it rip. Well, from that pitch on, he went on to win the Cy Young Award.

You can do the same. (But don't expect an award, because there are no awards in parenting.)

---

185. Take a good look at your baby's first steps.

That'll be the last time you see your kid walk. After those steps, first gear is obliterated from her shift box and she becomes a Corvette that goes from zero to sixty in five steps. When she was two, our daughter said, "I'm running so fast you can't hear my feet." That's pretty fast.

Just after our son learned to walk (run), he fractured his leg. Do you think a cast stopped him from running? No way! After a few weeks, pedestrians would stop to watch, their mouths open in wonder.

186. Stair alert.

Once your kid can walk, he quickly cranes his neck skyward and considers what heights he can scale—with much the same fervor as a climber getting his first look at K2 or Everest. You wish you could hand your kid some pitons and a rope, because when you get down on your belly and consider his perspective, your heart beats out of your chest.

Your kid knows when the time is right. Nostrils flared, eyes ablaze, he goes for it. You or your wife stands at the bottom of the stairs biting knuckles. Going up is one heck of a lot easier than going down, and your child knows it. He'll hesitate going down weeks after he's mastered going up.

When our daughter was learning stairs, we lived on the fourth floor of a walk-up brownstone. The stairs were perfect for tots: carpet, wide landings, easy turns, a banister, and plenty of rails. But our son had to learn in an elevator apartment building, which presented a challenge. We took him to the service stairs, but those were dank and dimly lit, so his real practice came on weekends, on the rackety, uncarpeted, steep stairs of our cottage—which was a bit like learning to ski on a giant slalom course before you've learned to snowplow. But, like any kid, he didn't mind.

Kids will fall down stairs. It's your job to be sure they don't get hurt. Socks on stairs are like black ice on a curvy country road, so try to have your kid wear those nifty socks with rubberized soles. Install gates. The best ones are wooden and have a metal clasp at one end and a swinging mechanism at the other.

187. When your year-old baby is zonked out in her stroller at three P.M., go to bed with your wife.

An afternoon is perfect for early-parenthood sex because your nerves aren't totally shot—as they invariably are by late night. Afternoon sex feels naughty. It feels young. That's great, because about right now you feel neither naughty nor young.

188. Install a lock on your bedroom door (or at least a hook to keep it shut).

You light a candle (which is like sending Morse code to your wife: s . . . e . . . x . . . s . . . e . . . x). Then, you wait for your child to go to sleep. Your wife reads her massive everything-you-could-ever-wonder-about-a-child-during-the-early-years tome and you flip aimlessly through a magazine. "Let's just be quiet and do it," you suggest. "No," she replies. "Wait."

You twiddle your thumbs. "Go check," she whispers. You tiptoe down the hall. Perfect slumber: teddy bear in arms, rapid eye movement under eyelids. You tiptoe back, close the door, dim the lights, quietly set her book on the floor so it doesn't wake the baby, pull off her glasses, pull off her top . . .

Then . . . *Code red! Little footsteps!* She yanks her top back on, you throw the covers back on, you reach for her book, and you both pretend to be reading in the dark.

Since there's no door lock, your little girl comes right in. "Whatadoin'?"

Get a lock.

189. Don't schedule sex.

Some books on fathering suggest you mark your calendar for when you and your wife plan to have sex, to make sure you can fit it into your hectic schedule. *Hmmm* . . . "Honey, what are we doing a week from Thursday?" "Isn't that the night we're having sex?" "I know that, but I was wondering if we could reschedule? I'm supposed to meet with the accountant about the audit, and you know how unhorny I get after I think about the IRS. What about two weeks from Thursday?" Yeah, surefire excitement.

Try this instead: On a not too crazy-busy day, start early, say, around noon, with a sexy call to your wife. Be subtle, but drop some hints—you know, the stuff you used to say when you were dating. When you get home, be extra sure to focus on her and your baby. Bring home some sensuous contribution to your dinner (avocado, an exotic fruit, steamer clams, olive oil—whatever she'd find sexy). Throw your newspaper in the recycling pile and don't drone on about your dreary day. Lie on your back and play airplane with your baby; ask your wife to join you.

When your baby is asleep, take a bath or a shower together. Resist the evening news. Don't read too long. Then, if one of you doesn't conk out, you may have some sex tonight.

190. Help your wife through weaning.

Your wife assumes there's a portion of your male soul that's just been waiting to have those knockers back—*all yours!* None of it is simple for her. She's pushed her baby into the world, but nursing was the last umbilical cord.

Understand she wouldn't be the first mother to go through nursing withdrawal. Be extra compassionate.

191. Your wife's breasts will probably be smaller than before she nursed your baby.

Be *very* careful of your wife's feelings. We were at a hotel poolside in Miami a year after my wife had stopped breast-feeding, quietly reading children's books and romping with our kids in the water, when a woman with show-stopping breasts walked slinkily toward the water, grabbed a raft, took off her orange bikini top, and floated breasts-up around the pool. All the guys in lounge chairs pretended to read magazines, but you could see their heads swivel in unison as she floated from the shallow end to the deep end and back.

I could tell my wife was looking down at her breasts (a touch less full after nursing our two kids), wondering if they still had their stuff. I said, "Just for the record: your breasts are perfect." Whatever you say, be sure to let her know that breast-feeding was a gift she gave to your child.

192. Pay special attention to your wife before she goes on a work trip.

That means get your sex life into high gear before she goes, romance the hell out of her, write a sincere love note and throw it into her suitcase so she'll discover it on the trip. All this helps inoculate her from the attentions of strangers sitting next to her on the plane—you know, the guys who are hitting on her and asking her out to dinner. It helps if she's still catching her breath from you.

When she's away, you want to be sure she knows everything's under control, but that she's missed. If things are too under control, she thinks, "They don't even know that I'm gone." But if chaos rules when she calls (the tub is overflowing, bath bubbles are now shoulder high—in other words, life is imitating a sitcom), call her back when there's a calm moment.

193. When your wife's away, find out what you're made of.

Whenever my wife goes away on business, her mother offers to help and my mother offers to help—but I decline their offers because I find it comforting to know I can manage for a short time alone with the kids. Sure, make an effort to keep it fun, but don't go for the easy wins, such as ice cream or candy. Keep the structure. No late bedtimes, or you'll pay for it tomorrow.

One thing nobody talks about much is how you'll feel when you've proved to yourself that you can not only survive but *thrive* with your kid(s) alone. That's the greatest gift of your wife's business trips.

194. Know you will miss your child when you travel.

There was a long period in my life when I felt I needed to nail my shoes into place in order not to hop the nearest plane for anywhere. Fatherhood changed all that. Now, one kiss blown through the receiver to me and I'm ready to return home. Once when I was away, my daughter got on the phone and said, "I got sick and Dr. Brown came over with his dog Harry and put down his bag and shot me in the fanny and I didn't even cry." (He's retired or I'd give you his telephone number.) I felt a clogging in my throat. After I hung up the phone, I lay awake, wishing I were there.

6 TIPS FOR YOUR BUSINESS TRIPS

1. Keep your business trips brief, and get back soon.
2. Tell your kids when you'll be going and when you'll be

back. Tape a note to the fridge so they can cross off the days if they're old enough.

3. Call home when they're certain to be there (say, breakfast or dinner).
4. Leave a note behind for each nighttime. Be sure to write how much you miss your child, and add hugs and kisses (your wife can read it aloud).
5. Arrange with your wife to have your child call you.
6. Don't get locked into major gift buying on trips, but bring something back. T-shirts make great nightshirts when the kids are little.

---

195. Decide if you and your wife will take the same airplane.

Even though you know the chance of your plane going down is less than the chance of your car getting in a wreck en route to the airport, your mind is plagued by *what if . . .*

My friends Eric and Veronica, new parents leaving their child at home for the first time, took separate planes to Vail. But one day into the trip, they found themselves swinging over a thousand-foot precipice in a ski lift gondola that had lost its power. Eric turned to his wife and said, "What were we thinking‽! The plane's nothing compared to this!"

They rode the same plane back home. (But what you and your wife do is a choice you have to discuss way before you buy the tickets.)

196. Have a water fight with your wife—or a snowball fight or roll down a grassy slope or make a fire and roast marshmallows.

All that stuff you did when you were courting is important to your marriage, now that you're Ma and Pa.

197. Know when it's time to take your wife to a hotel.

One way to tell is when you sleep so far away from one another that you're both nearly falling off the bed. When one of you says, "Good night," the other grunts or says, "Uhmmm."

Without a doubt, it's time you pick up the phone and call the nearest hotel or motel. Forget the cash. You can't keep a marriage (and a sex life) afloat going out to movies and dinner. You need a chunk of time to get . . . well, reacquainted.

The hotel receptionist might wink when you give your home address, as if this woman, your wife, is a mistress. Great: That means you're sending off the right signals to your wife and nobody can believe you're married (much less parents). Say, "We're just taking a night away from the kids." Those are magic words. You might just get a free upgrade, because the world loves anyone who tries to beat the odds and stay happily, lustily, head-over-heels married.

Bring a bottle or two of wine, maybe some new lingerie, whatever else will turn your wife on. Don't act like a tourist. This is not a sightseeing trip.

(The sights you see are *in* the room.) Get to the gym, if the hotel has one, work out, take a steam or sauna, undo the stress of normal life. Tip your schedule upside down: Stay up late, sleep late, eat late—you get the picture.

Then, when you're at the door to your home, pause to kiss your wife the way you used to. Let her know she'll always be your lover.

TRY TO GO ON AT LEAST ONE SLEEPOVER WITH YOUR WIFE EACH YEAR.

---

198. Create a peaceful home.

Try not to fight in front of your baby or child. Imagine how it must sound: like the two of you are going to hurt one another. A peaceful home might also include not talking about work problems incessantly, not watching the TV news (or violent shows) in front of your child, or not allowing friends to come over and say things in front of your child that he's not ready to hear.

Once you create the right environment, departures from it seem more obvious—and it becomes natural to nip them in the bud.

199. Know how, when, and where to argue.

Before your baby was on the scene, you could turn your home into a private fighting arena. Those days are gone forever. Now, there's wide-eyed Baby, who is always ready to throw a fit to match your own.

Men like to hammer it out, then make it okay (or pay the penalty). Think of Billy Martin barking into an umpire's face, throwing his cap, and kicking dirt on home plate. But your child will be freaked out by your raised voices. So don't fight in front of him. A lot of fights start innocently enough, and you two are just getting into it when it dawns on you both that the little wide-eyed creature in the high chair is watching.

Learn to postpone your fights. Give each other a hug to demonstrate to your child that life is full of disagreements and *resolutions.* By doing so, you defuse the situation and drain all the emotionality out of it. Later, you can see the outlines of the disagreement more clearly.

The absolutely wrong time to fight is four A.M. Your baby cries; you growl that you got up once before; your wife says she got up twice; you say you have a meeting at ten A.M.; she says she has one at one P.M. You're vying to see who's worse off so you don't have to get up when . . . *shunnnk!* You throw an emotional dagger that's meant to wound. It does. She reels back and lets fly a poisoned emotional arrow. *Boiing!* This continues until one of you gets up and feeds the baby, then you, thoroughly pissed off, march out to the living room couch, where you dream of the Perfect Young Thing who worships *everything* about you. When you go back to the bedroom to mumble your apology, your wife is snoring (or pretending to) and you can't sleep because you feel rotten. A lot of good that fight did you.

200. Avoid the Angry Swoop.

You hear a problem brewing in another room. It escalates. Louder. You're drumming your fingers, unable to focus on anything but what's happening next door. You wait. Your wife seems to be doing nothing. Suddenly, you burst in the other room, shout, "Okay, that's enough now!" and angrily swoop up your kid. But you do it too quickly, with excess vigor, and your baby cries and your wife asks why you couldn't be more gentle.

Better to say, "Hey, you need some help in there?" If she does, walk to the next room and have her hand you the baby.

201. Be careful of car travel blowups.

You're driving along and the traffic stops, creating a seven-mile parking lot. Your baby wakes up. No more good vibrations. You clench the wheel. You grind your teeth. The radio is telling you your mutual fund portfolio is down 20 percent. You check your watch. You look in the rearview mirror and see your baby is gearing up for a good long cry. What to do?

If there's spare time, take the next exit and go to the nearest distraction, be it a McDonalds with a play gym, a truck stop with mini-juke boxes, or a pond with ducks.

Here's another remedy: Pull over and let your wife drive, throw headphones over your ears, crank up the Allman Brothers' "Whipping Post," and say to yourself (but not your wife), "I'm there."

202. Recover from your meltdown.

There are two types of meltdowns: rational and irrational. A rational meltdown is when a car clips the corner so closely it nearly hits you and your baby. A nuclear blast goes off in your chest. You yell raspy-voiced obscenities. If you were to catch the offending driver, you'd yank him through his barely opened window and shake him against the pavement. Later, you tell your wife and she hugs you for your protective instinct.

An irrational meltdown is uglier: It's when you overreact to a not-so-terrible situation. For instance, the baby's crying in the back car seat unhinges you, so you pull over, get out, and violently kick a car tire or a nearby tree—until your wife says, "Somebody's going to institutionalize you!" You stop. She's right. You immediately want to dig a hole in the earth and crawl in.

Losing it is *never* a good idea. But fatherhood does (for whatever reason) put you in closer touch with your rage. If you have a meltdown, get up, dust yourself off, give your wife and kid a kiss, apologize profusely, take a few steps back, and try again. You'll make it.

HAVE FAMILY MEETINGS. Sure, your child is a bit young to vent his views, but having regular family meetings is a great habit. Form it now. Later, when the going gets rough, it'll help to let everyone air their thoughts. Say, "Okay, we're having a family meeting."

The rules are simple. One person talks first. Nobody interrupts. Then each person has a turn. Usually, by the time you've gone around a few times, there's a new peacefulness in the air. You'll feel like a dad in control.

---

203. Take a step back and see the big picture.

Right: That's not always so easy. On a particularly tough day of parenting, bring out your photo albums and look at them with your wife and child. Or watch a few of your earliest home videos. Children are mezmerized by seeing themselves as infants. Fill in the blanks in your child's memory with recollections of what it was like back then.

Sometimes that's all it takes for you, your wife, and child to have a sense of moving through time together.

204. *Take responsibility if you have to move.*

Yes, it's a major pain, but sometimes you've got to move. We moved twice when our babies were young: once because we had a four-flight walk-up and our toddler took twenty minutes navigating the stairs, another time after our son was born and we needed more room. Take charge. Best if you get your wife to take the baby away while the old home is being disassembled; it's very upsetting to your kid. Even more important that you reassemble your baby's belongings in her new digs before she sees them. After all, your child's home is the stuff inside put together in a particular way.

When your child is older, be sure to bring her back to her first home. From outside, point to the room that was her nursery and say, "That was your room. You slept there the night we brought you home from the hospital." When she says, "Really?" you'll have an irresistible urge to hug your kid.

205. *Don't laugh when your baby does an imitation of Dustin Hoffman as "Mumbles."*

He's been trying out sounds for a while, but now the sounds are interconnected into singsong rambles. "Dat-dat-dat-dat-dat . . . na-na-na!" What makes it doubly difficult is that he knows what he means to say (you don't) and he's waiting for your reply.

So, answer these mumbled paragraphs! Make it fun and you'll both end up giggling.

206. *Devise a secret language with your kid.*

My one-and-a-half-year-old son would be sitting in his high chair, yogurt dripping everywhere off his spoon. I'd walk in the room and make a lion's growl. *R-cchhh-rrr.* He'd look up from his mess and go, *Rrrr-cchhh-rrr.* Nobody knew what it meant except us. To me, it meant, "Hey, dude. I'd like to eat that way, too, but I can't get away with it." His reply meant something like, "Huh . . . and I thought I was doing a pretty close imitation of the way you eat!"

The lion call really worked for us. Try something like it.

207. Use your shoulders.

Kids love being "the tallest"—that's where your shoulders come in. You become a human lookout tower as you strut along, and your kid feels like part of your body. Enjoy it. It's one of the treats of being a dad. (And it will open up special worlds—like the time the movie projectionist invites you in his room for a tour because he saw your kid's excited face gleaming through his window.)

208. Have you read **Curious George** *yet?*

Your kid is, in essence, a monkey that will get in trouble no matter what he does. A toddler will play with every knob on your car dash, so when you turn the ignition, your car stereo nearly blows the upholstery off the seats and every light is blinking and beeping.

Half the battle with toddlers is keeping things safe enough so they can make tolerable mischief. You don't want to hover too much. Lend your glass coffee table to a friend who has no kids, yank out precarious bookcases (or bolt them to the wall), tighten the locks on cabinets, keep your shaving razor out of reach. Your kid is testing his physical limits and he'll keep doing that—and that's all right. Think of your adolescence: Remember riding a sled charioteer-style down an icy hill? (I do.) As a parent, you're saying, I can't move the trees, but I'm just making sure there's not a busy road at the bottom of the slope.

209. Frame your kid's art.

Nothing fancy. Those plastic clip-together frames are great because you can change the art easily and often. Designate a kid's art wall in your home.

If you frame some of your kid's art in a nice wooden frame and bring it to your office, people might assume it's modern art. Good. Watch them blush when you tell them your kid made it.

BE SURE TO WRITE THE DATE AND YOUR CHILD'S NAME ON THE BACK OF HIS ARTWORKS. Store the art in a flat box or drawer, but don't bother saving stuff that will disintegrate or come unglued (like pasta art). Your child's descriptions (especially of an abstract painting) can be especially enlightening. Write them on the back, too.

---

210. Get musical instruments.

Babies are born percussionists. Early on, plastic eggs filled with beads are best. Buy some at a music store and your baby will love how the sensation in his hand is tied to the sound in his ear. Later, you can pull out the pots and pans, but real drums are cooler. Best to get some cheapies—the baby might poke the drum stick right through. Flea markets usually have some big, old drums that look great hung on a wall when they're not being used. And, get enough sticks so you can hammer along, too.

We got an old piano that the kids pounded on, too. But my real find was an old Silvertone guitar I found sticking out of a trash can in New York City. I could hardly believe my eyes when I lifted it out: a mini-guitar for my kids (also a collectible). What more could a kid want than the *power* of an electric guitar?

211. Limit computer use.

Yes, it's terrific that your child enjoys a reading program CD-ROM and has mastered use of the mouse. But too much time at the computer shuts down your kid's ability to entertain himself, so set limits. At this age, a paintbrush in a kid's hand is better than a keyboard at his fingertips.

212. Become a dictator of TV programming.

You won't feel too bad during your kid's early TV-watching years, when he watches nothing but public television. *Sesame Street* introduces your child to the little girl who helps run a Mexican bakery and the boy who collects water for his African family. Some of the shows help with spelling, numbers, and geography. The station itself helps limit the amount your child watches: no two-year-old wants to see an advanced math show at 6:30 A.M.

But once he's moved into the Technicolor world of cartoons, it's a lot harder to control your kid's TV intake. You cringe at the violence. You detest the commercials. Suddenly, all your kid wants to watch is a coyote splatter himself in every conceivable way. So what do you do?

You buy a slew of videos. Some are educational. Others are Disney.

The photon blast seduces your kid into a Zen-like trance, minus the spirituality. You feel your authority slip. Until . . .

One day, you put your foot down. But how? First, determine how much TV you think your kid should watch. Then, limit TV intake. If you have more than one TV in the house, stash the extra(s) in a closet. Limit days or hours that your kid can watch. Try alternating days or weeks. You might decide that your child can watch on weekend mornings and evenings, but not on weekdays. Place a timer near the TV, and turn off the set when you hear a *ding.* Turn off the TV any time there's a tantrum (or a sibling fight).

If you feel none of these intermediary measures are working, try no TV for a month. This will not be a popular decision with your kid (I know firsthand), but the charm of life without TV becomes almost instantly apparent—even to your child. It's quieter, more peaceful and harmonious. You hear more laughter, giggles, games, and play. The pets get attention. Your kid finds more frogs, builds more forts, and takes more walks in the rain.

An August with no TV is, well, bliss.

213. Never watch the news with your kid in the room.

214. Know the Blue Jeans Rule.

If you're not getting holes in the knees of your jeans, it means you're not getting down to your kid's height. Which means your kid is staring up into your hairy nostrils. Which isn't a pleasant view.

TUNE IN. Look for the "zone" in fatherhood, just as you do playing basketball (when the hoop seems ten feet wide) or baseball (when the ball looks big as a watermelon). You'll be playing on your knees with your kid or reading to him at night when *whammo!* There it is: You feel really right as a dad. Don't let it slip by unnoticed.

215. Let your imagination fly.

The best games my kids and I played were always the ones we made up on the spot. Like Igloo: Take all the pillows from your beds and make a pile over you and then pretend you're in the freezing Arctic with penguins, polar bears, and piercing winds for companions. Or Raft: Get on your bed with your kids and pretend there are dolphins, sharks, and whales in the water (your bedroom floor); one of you falls overboard and the others pull the water-bound one back on board. Or Puppy: Your kid pretends he's a puppy in a store and you walk in, choose him, and walk him home. Or North Woods: Get under the covers with your kid with a flashlight. Tell all those camping stories you were told. If you shut off your rationality, you might feel as transported as your child.

216. Tell nighttime stories.

Talk about an adoring audience! You can watch your toddler's eyes sparkle as you wind up the sort of tale you imagine you'd have liked as a child. Stay on your kid's turf (nothing that starts, "There was once a hardworking prince in Silicon Valley . . . "). And no obvious morality tales about well-behaved children: Kids see through that stuff. Just a good old adventure with a beginning, middle, and end. Time your tales so the story's curtain falls just as your child's eyes close. Then, a kiss on the forehead, tiptoe out of the room, and a declaration of love from the doorway.

Don't be afraid to repeat a story. Kids don't have a problem with repetition.

217. Enroll in a kid course—and go with your kid.

Sure, it'll be just you and the mommies and the nannies and a bunch of eighteen-month-old babies, but you'll have a ball. Call up a children's museum about art classes or ask about music classes, or gymnastics classes. Find a class that meets once a week and be sure it's the type of class where you'll be banging away at the instruments or tumbling on the mats or flinging paint on paper (no dad-on-the-sidelines stuff). Wear a T-shirt, jeans, and sneakers—your jacket and tie are for the office.

P.S. A baby course is a great place to find a nanny or baby-sitter, too.

218. Kids aren't fragile.

One day, I saw a magazine photo of a Russian mother standing waist deep in frigid, icy, winter waters, about to dunk her infant in for an invigorating dip. I'm not saying you ought to go to that extreme (your wife will institutionalize you!), but I am saying you don't have to pussyfoot around with your kid, either.

One night, I wanted to go skiing at our local slopes. I asked, "Anybody want to join me?" My nearly three-year-old son said, "Yeah, sure!" Jumping off her chair, my wife said, "Why would anyone want to ski when it's minus five degrees outside?" I looked at my son; he looked at me. "I guess because we're guys," I said.

There was hardly one centimeter of his soft skin exposed to the wind and cold that night, and we took only two quick runs, but I'll never forget snowplowing him down the slopes, all bundled up like Eskimos. Or later, in the lodge, playing with those little marshmallows in our hot chocolates, our feet up near the roaring fire.

There are moments when you realize how empty your life would be if not for your child. You pinch yourself: Was this the baby I carried out of the hospital? Amazing . . .

219. Know the reproductive patterns of your child's pets.
Our kids were elated to have "boy" and "girl" gerbils. However, they produced so many offspring that we thought we were going to have to open a pet shop.

Before you buy a pet, find out about the peeing and pooping patterns of the species, too. And don't trust the pet store salesman; ours told us we would have to clean the guinea pig cage "once a month." If we had waited that long, the department of sanitation would have broken down our doors to find out why the neighbors couldn't breathe.

220. Don't become slaves to your kids.
Do your kids seem to have you hopping over coals to get them a drink when they want it, how they want it, in what cup they want it? Be careful not to spoil them: It's not a favor, it's a curse.

How can you maintain yourself without becoming a bad father? Set limits in advance, discuss them with your wife, notify your child, give warnings, then stick to your rules. Establish positive rewards so you don't feel like you're constantly saying "No!" Make a conscious effort to also say "Yes!" And don't forget to pat your kid on the back and say, "You're amazing!" or ask, "How could I have been so lucky to be your father?"

Enough said. End of lecture. Good luck! (And, yeah, I hate to see my kid unhappy, too.)

5. TALKING DAYS: The Third Year

221. Rejoice! You're just starting to get your brain cells back!

222. Don't believe in the Terrible Twos.

The great soothsayers who call themselves your friends and acquaintances really come out to haunt you on this one! My wife and I were terrified that our little paradise would be lost when the clock struck midnight on our daughter's second birthday.

We waited . . . and waited . . . but nothing happened. We still loved our new parenthood, and our daughter didn't turn into a monster, as predicted.

As it turned out, the only terrible thing was the many predictions.

DON'T ABANDON TAG TEAM PARENTING. It worked with your infant, and it'll work with your toddler, too.

---

223. *Get ready for the Little Communicator.*

Many guys I know admitted they weren't totally sold on fatherhood until their child started talking. Your child's ability to use words in complete sentences happens around the second year, and that's when you get a glimpse into your kid's mind.

"I wish babies were born being able to speak," my cousin Bennett said, "because until then, I felt sort of like a third wheel. Finally, I got into it." My friend Bjorn said, "I remember when early fatherhood was totally satisfying in a way that nothing had been before. I was in an elevator that had zero for the ground floor and one for the first floor and minus one for the basement. I was going up and down, explaining to my kid the nature of numbers."

224. *Hold your ground.*

You'll bring home a box of chocolates, not realizing the storm of negotiation you'll have to go through. Your kid: "How many?" You: "One." Kid: "One?" You: "One." Kid: "One now and one later?" You: "One." Kid: "One small one and one big one?" You: "One." Kid (holding up her doll): "One for me and one for my doll?" You: "One." And on and on.

The problem is, once you define your ground, you can't budge—or you damage your bargaining power in all future negotiations. (Don't you wish you were half as tough negotiating at work?)

WHEN ALL ELSE FAILS, SAY, "THOSE ARE THE RULES." For whatever reason, kids hear a clap of thunder and see a bolt of lightning when you say, "Those are the rules." It's as if you're saying, "The rules are beyond my control. Nothing can be done. Accept it."

Don't cite The Rules too often, or the gesture loses its power.

---

225. Organize a second birthday party.

This one will really count, because your baby did little but smudge the chocolate cake over her face at her first birthday and now your toddler knows *exactly* what's happening: *They're celebrating me!!!* Our daughter wore her favorite gold slippers and acted like a princess inviting guests to her castle (a kiddie gym).

All the experts tell you to invite one guest for each year of your child's age. *Two guests?* Yeah, right . . . We invited half as many people as were at our wedding—but we had twice as much fun.

Basically, there are three parts of any child's birthday party: Before Cake, During Cake, and After Cake. It's sort of like watching a NASA takeoff on TV: there's the countdown, ignition, and liftoff. Especially if During Cake happens to be chocolate, the kids will go stonily quiet . . . and then they explode into fervent, heated motion. Keep After Cake time to a minimum, or the boys will begin sword fighting with the plastic forks. You want the party to end before tears.

Take pictures and videos—especially of blowing out the candles, which is enough to make a hardened criminal go misty. Do *not* entrust your video camera to a child (as I once did) or you'll need Pepto-Bismol when you're watching later on.

I know—guys aren't supposed to have a sentimental bone in their bodies, but those early birthday parties really choked me up. I think back on them often, wishing they'd return, but they won't, so appreciate them now.

226. Redecorate your child's room.

Use your imagination, and this time, get your kid's input, too.

227. Keep a wish list of things you want to do with your child.

Tack it to the inside of your closet so you don't lose sight of your dreams. Mine included taking my kids skating under the stars, sitting with my kids at a day game in Wrigley Field, teaching my kids to jump off a rope swing into our local pond, camping out and roasting marshmallows, night skiing and having hot chocolate in a lodge, running alongside my kid as he learned to ride a bike, letting go, and watching him take off on his own.

But actually it's the little unplanned stuff that takes you by storm: the time you stop in a rain shower under a bridge in the park and yell, "Echo-echo-echo . . . ," and watch your kid's face light up in wonder. The time you hold your child's tiny body and slide her down a stair rail over and over and over. The time you and your little son wake up before dawn, and you toss him up on your shoulders and hike to a spot to see the sun come up.

228. Take your kid to the ball game.

When my daughter was six months old, I took her to Yankee Stadium to fulfill my longtime dream. I managed to fall onto the grass in pursuit of a batting practice grounder (and got it autographed for her), sang the national anthem and "Take Me Out to the Ball Game" with my baby pressed to my chest, and had my wife photograph me, the euphoric dad with his kid on his lap as he's taking in the game and every type of junk food known to man.

Over the years, I've also enjoyed bringing my kids to minor league games out in the cornfields of New York state, where the kid-to-adult ratio in the stands is a pleasant four-to-one, there's enough kitsch for a Hollywood movie, and it doesn't much matter who wins. But the pinnacle of my baseball watching career came one clear September day at Wrigley Field, my son on my shoulders, the crowd chanting "Samm-y! Sammmm-y!!" and Sosa popping one into the hands of a Bleacher Bum in the right field stands for number fifty-six, then rounding the bases, tapping home, tipping his cap, blowing kisses to the fans and to his mother in the Dominican Republic, and returning for a curtain call. There's nobody in the world I'd rather have been with than my son.

My tips: Go early for batting practice, buy a beanie-bag souvenir, bring mitts and a ball (when your kid is old enough to play catch) . . . and monitor your intake of junk food some other time.

229. Buy your kid's first baseball bat and ball.

Here's one of the thrilling moments of fatherhood: tossing your first pitches to your kid, watching him whiff, shouting the encouraging words you heard when you were a kid: "Keep your eye on the ball" and "Wait for your pitch" and "Don't swing for the fences!"

Wiffle balls and bats are good, but the new Fred Flintstone-esque bat/caveman club is even better. Be ready to smile at hordes of mothers in the park who yell, "How cute!" at you and Junior.

Later, get out your old Louisville Slugger that's all weathered and nicked with scars from clobbered homers. *One day, this tattered toothpick will be yours . . .* (And he'll ask, "Gee, Dad, who was Rod Carew?")

P.S. While you're at it, get a basketball, soccer ball, and football for your kid, too.

230. Play at the playground.

Get in the sandbox and dig, zip down that slide, push your child on a swing, then get on one, too. Play tag and be sure to act winded as you tear after your kid. Use the playground as a break from work.

Maybe you've forgotten how much fun all this stuff is (I know I had). Besides, it's another excuse to be a child all over again by being a dad.

231. Be prepared for playground accidents.

There's a game I used to play with my high school buddies where one of us would bark out, "What would you do if you were mountain climbing and a snake bit you on the hand?" Then we'd rattle off our surefire remedy. Don't go to that extreme, but think ahead what you would do if your kid had an accident on the playground—because he probably will.

My then-toddler son and I were playing tag when, dashing gleefully, he pushed an iron gate with all his might and it ricocheted back into his head, the prong latch digging into his forehead. He turned to me, frozen; blood was gushing over his face.

Here's what you do: Hug your child, say he's going to be okay, take off your shirt, press it tightly to the wound, pull it off for an instant to examine the damage, then pick him up and get him to the nearest emergency room.

Through tears, he'll stammer, "I'm b-b-bleeding!" Never lie. Say, "Yes, but you're going to be okay." Any kid who knows he has to go to the emergency room will panic (and maybe dry heave). It's up to you to calm him.

The quality you should exude isn't all that different from when you were there with your wife during delivery. Steady. Strong. Trustworthy. When you get to the hospital, explain to the check-in attendant what happened and ask if a plastic surgeon is on duty. It's costlier, so check if it's covered by your insurance. But when you're staring at your child's face, all you want is to minimize the scar.

Children often get preference at emergency rooms, partly because it's so disturbing for adults to see a child crying or whimpering or shrieking. For a kid, the wait at the emergency room is almost worse than the actual visit with the doctor.

After he's examined, there will be an injection of painkiller near the wound and surgical gown fabric will be placed over the surrounding area. Stay with your child always. Hold his hand, place your head near his, and whisper consoling things. I said, "I'm bringing you to *Hercules on Ice.* Who do you want to see?" "Meg," he mumbled (referring to Hercules's sexy heartthrob). "Will she be there?" "You bet. We'll see Meg." That sort of thing.

Afterward, be sure to tell everyone how brave your kid was—and he'll pipe up with his own version of what happened. He'll also sleep like a rock that night, but you may need to tip back a beer or two to relax.

My son's scar is gone, but not the bond we formed that day.

232. Don't beat yourself up over mistakes.

The temptation is to replay your daddy mistakes endlessly in the projector of your mind. Don't. Move on. You can't be a parent and not make mistakes. Besides, while you're obsessing over the past, you're missing the present.

DON'T ACCIDENTALLY LEAVE YOUR KID BEHIND. I used to wonder about the central premise of the *Home Alone* movies (I'd think, *What kind of parent would inadvertently leave his kid behind¿*). Until I had kids. We once accidentally left our kid behind in Customs. (I nearly jumped out of my skin at the realization—and ran the fastest fifty-yard dash of my life when retrieving him!) But I've since heard many stories of parents who sat down in restaurants and began ordering their meal—only to realize (with a pang of horror) that they'd left their kid in his car seat. (They, too, escaped without damage.)

These mistakes come from being overly inundated—but there's really no excuse. So don't let it happen to you.

---

233. *Accept the fact that you're not going to adore being a father every minute.*

Men usually hold it in and pretend everything's all right when it's not. Ask most men about being a father and they say, "It's great! I love it!" Maybe they do, but not every minute. Here's the truth: It's like anything else, good one minute, terrible the next, boring for lots of it.

234. *Don't value your possessions over your kid.*

Kids wreak havoc on things—it just comes with the territory. When I wasn't looking, my toddler son began banging my electric guitar against the floor as though he were Hendrix at Monterey. So I grabbed it back and asked him what he was doing. He said, very plausibly, "I want to wake everyone in the house!" (which will probably be his impulse until he's eighteen).

If you're that worried, put it out of harm's way.

235. Don't go into Pork Out Mode with kid food.

One of the toughest aspects of fatherhood is being reintroduced to the foods of childhood. You suddenly find yourself shoveling down your kids' half-eaten oily brand peanut butter (the good-tasting type) and strawberry jelly (the sugary, good-tasting type) sandwich or slices of pizza (the tasty cheap-mozzarella-and-sugary-tomato-paste type) or spooned-until-it's-soup ice cream—and sometimes all three in rapid succession.

Whenever my wife catches me indulging in such kiddie food, she'll ask, "Why are you eating that?" "It's obvious," I'll reply. "Obvious?" she'll say. "Yeah," I'll say, "I'm after instant gratification at the expense of the future." But what she doesn't quite understand is, like many men, I've been "full" only a few times in my entire life (not counting Thanksgiving dinners). It's not easy to resist.

Now, I try to keep a stringent rule: no kiddie food. For me, it's easier than having to stop once I'm on a kiddie food binge.

236. Make a kiddie dining table.

Buy a cheap, portable card table, then saw the legs so they're fifteen inches high—the perfect height to accommodate little kiddie chairs. Be sure to place the rubber end caps on the new mini-table legs so you don't gouge your floors.

When you have a dinner party, invite the kids to eat nearby at their own table—and bring peace to meals. Kids love to pretend they're adults.

237. Prepare for tantrums in the grocery aisles.

You're zipping up and down aisles, your child gleefully navigating your course from the Kiddie Control Seat, when you pass the candy rack or the chips rack or the soda rack or the ice cream case that is always a magnetic lure for kids. "No," you say, igniting a riot. Everything happens at once. Your kid tosses the mayonnaise. It explodes. Crying. Tears. Hollering. Suddenly, everyone eyes you: *Who's that evil dad and what did he do to terrify that beautiful toddler?* A kind clerk mops up the mayomess, but all shopping has ceased until everyone knows what you did to your child! "No means no," you say firmly. Invariably, a stranger will poke her face into the fray: "Oh, quit being so hard on her. Kids love chocolate. Here." She hands her the chocolate.

Gee, thanks.

Put yourself in your kid's shoes. Imagine the frustration. You can't do anything well enough for the adults, you're not really a baby, but you still can't sit on the potty, you can't swim or hit a baseball or write or read or tell time—still, you *feel* very big. So what do you do? What any toddler would do: cry, throw things, spit, hit, swing, kick, toss mayonnaise jars out of carts.

What's really frightening is that you know you're getting a taste of what's to come: zitty, rebellious, rip-up-the-flag adolescence. Charming, no?

238. Know there are two types of toddlers: those who behave better at home and are monsters in public and those who are monsters at home and behave better in public.

Take your choice. Either you've got a great home life but everyone thinks you've got a Baby from Hell, or you've got a Baby from Hell and everyone tells you she's an angel.

239. Don't buy tons of expensive toys.

The consumer society will begin to seduce you and your baby soon after he leaves the bassinet. *Buy the toy that he wants and he'll have happiness! Buy it and you'll have peace and quiet!*

At the toy store, your kid will spot the bright red propeller plane that appears to fly high above the houses, soaring amidst the clouds, zooming through trees. All for twenty bucks! You can't open the box until you buy it, and the lady behind the counter says, "The box says it flies, so it flies," and your kid is screaming, "I want it to fly!" so you shell out the dough and get home and . . . discover it's got a pull cord and a battery-operated motor that sounds like a sneaker thudding about in a dryer—but it doesn't fly. Now there's toddler despair. *Make it fly!* Then he throws it into the air, it nose-dives, the propeller breaks off, and you can't return it.

Actually, the best toys are found in nature or in your home. Get a handful of berries and roll them toward a target. Give your kid two ladles, water, and a pot. Or some simple stacking cups and a ball. You and your kid can play with these things for hours, improvising upon the rules to keep it interesting.

Most of the expensive, intricate toys you buy in a store will bore your child sooner than you think.

240. Your parents may be a lot better at being grandparents than they were as your mom and dad.

241. Exploit Grandma's and Grandpa's talents.

I'm the sort of guy who breaks into a sweat when he has to assemble his child's crib. So imagine my terror when I watch my kid open a birthday gift that has two zillion moving parts and an instruction manual thicker than a car's. *Ahhhhh!!* I freeze and feel . . . inept.

But I realized that my father, who is one of the most technologically minded men I've ever known, was made for the job. I've learned to stash away all the high-tech gifts for his visits; then, I put him to work. Amazingly, everyone's happy: The kids see Grandpa as a dashing hero who wields a screwdriver and hammer with the greatest of ease, and Grandpa hears the magic words: thank you. And I feel that wonderful sensation of being sandwiched between the two generations.

242. Now that you know how hard it is to raise a child, tell your parents that you finally appreciate what they went through with you.

If you really want to make amends, write them a note and tell them what you've discovered being a dad. Use plain old English; tell them how you feel. You're sure to get a sobby, appreciative phone call. You might even hear your own parents say they admire you as a parent, which will take your breath away.

One day, if you're lucky, your own kid will e-mail the same feelings to you—and you (like your parents now) will say to your wife, "I guess we did okay."

SAY TO YOUR WIFE, "THE MOST MAVERICK THING WE CAN DO IS STAY MARRIED AND HAVE A GREAT FAMILY." (She'll love you for saying it!) Create a sense of daring: Dare yourselves to stay happily married; dare yourselves to turn heads by how much fun you have as a family.

243. Keep your sex life spicy.

When I was in high school, my grandmother somehow pilfered my copy of *The Happy Hooker* and came down for breakfast one morning in a foul mood. "Well," she said, clearly disturbed, "in my day, we used whipped cream on ice cream sundaes." I turned beet red as she lobbed my book back to me.

Sex *has* changed. My friend Annette put it rather bluntly: "My husband and I have a great sex life. We have fun. We get dressed up. We get kinky. We play-act. I've got a dresser drawer filled with sexy things and so does he. We go for it. We try to keep being a couple separate from being parents."

Do you remember how on your honeymoon, or soon thereafter, you and your wife pledged never to be like everyone else and slide into sexual apathy? Before becoming parents, you might have been pretty good at keeping this promise. Slowly, though, you lost your momentum. Remember when you used to kiss each other every night before going to sleep? Or hug first thing in the morning? Or sneak a hand under her blouse and slip fingers under her bra?

Start incorporating those little gestures back into your life. Then, see what you can do to break up the complacent routine of your sex life. Remember: Your sex life is what differentiates your relationship with your wife from your relationship with everyone else. You never want your wife to say, "My husband and I are like train tracks—running parallel paths, but never touching." Pay attention to your wife daily.

244. Tell your wife when it's really good.

Sooner or later, you and your wife will have the same mind-blowing sex you used to have before you became parents. Cosmic sex. You'll feel as if you've been to another planet and back.

Every new mother wants to know that she still casts a spell over you. Tell her that the sex you just had was not only as good as before—it was better.

You can finally laugh at your obsession over whether sex would ever be the same. Now you know what women generally understand: It's different every time.

245. Internet porno will not turn your wife on.

One new father recounted how he lugged his laptop to bed to show his wife Internet porno. "Check out this photo," he said, hoping to stimulate her interest. She said, "Yuck. Get it away!" "It doesn't turn you on?" he asked. "No. Look at her nails, her polish, and her earrings," she said. "Her nails, polish, and earrings?!" he replied. His wife continued, "Those claws are disgusting. And so are those marbles hanging from her earlobes. What a turnoff!"

Next time, he tried some erotic stories (nothing that described the woman's nails or her earrings). This didn't work either.

246. Go to bed at the same time your wife does.

One sure way to ensure No Sex is for your wife to get in bed at ten P.M., while you stay up to catch a ball game and a late-night show in the living room. Do you really want your wife to think you're little more than a diaper-changing partner?

247. Get a balance board.

You probably haven't seen one since you were a kid. Remember? It's a board that fits over a cylinder and you're meant to balance on top. Well, standing on a balance board is just like fatherhood. You're being pulled this way and pushed that way, and you're liable to lose your center. A balance board teaches you to stay steady. You suck in your gut, distribute your weight evenly, and find stability.

I use my balance board whenever I'm watching a ball game. It becomes almost effortless, but I feel a pleasant tightness in my inner legs and gut whenever I'm done.

Your kids will love to try, too. Put a stable chair next to it so they can hold on to the chair back. Place the cylinder on a fluffy towel so it's not as wobbly. They'll try every day until they master it, too.

10 WAYS FATHERHOOD WILL CHANGE YOU FOR THE BETTER:

1. You'll be more solid and dependable.
2. You'll be more focused and organized.

3. You'll be more productive at work in less time.
4. You'll stop hanging out with useless people.
5. You'll take fewer unnecessary risks.
6. You'll get by on less sleep.
7. You'll learn to manage your worries.
8. You'll have less sex but more love.
9. You'll be less consumed with the small, stupid stuff in life.
10. You'll realize that being a father fulfills your role as a man.

---

248. No, you can't stop buying diapers now.

Your kid will seem to take forever to get with the toilet program (although little girls can be wonderfully precocious in this regard). All the experts can make your head spin: Potty train too early or too late and you cause problems. You buy the requisite books, read them to your child, and set a potty out but don't insist your child use it. By then, you and your wife have been through so many phases you feel like hurdlers who've already cleared a dozen gates and know you can somehow get over this, too.

Call your child's pediatrician for advice. Patience is key.

249. Boys and girls are different, too.

If you have one of each, just ask your wife how a boy baby nurses differently from a girl baby (the boy acts as though he's just crossed the Sahara, while the girl looks as if she's having tea sandwiches and listening to waltzes). Well, a boy toddler is different, too. For one thing, he'll wear right through his sneakers, while a girl toddler can wear her silver slippers for a year.

I was at a state fair trying my damnedest to win a yellow-and-pink teddy bear for my adoring little girl, and I didn't care what it cost me to win that $1.29 piece of gaudy fuzz. But years later, when I brought my son to the same fair, he wanted to out-sledgehammer me in getting the metal ball to *ding* the bell on the pole.

Enjoy the difference.

250. Never criticize your daughter's weight.

It starts early, before you even know advertising messages are reaching your child. You're pushing her in a stroller and she's suddenly face-to-face with a blue jeans ad on the side of a bus. Your daughter is now studying a picture of a rail-thin woman, scantily clad, sometimes not even showing her jeans. The billboard's subliminal message is *Eat celery and drink water and you'll be sexy*.

One comment about your daughter's weight can do irreparable damage, so use extreme caution. Later, you'll be shocked at how eight-year-old girls obsess over their weight.

251. Pee with your boy.

Sure, it's sexist—it's something you can't do with your daughter. But all it takes is a backyard and full bladders and you've got an instant good time. My little son would try to see who could pee further or see if he could aim at a leaf and hit it or make an arc and say, "Rainbow!"

Toilet peeing is to outdoor peeing what indoor baseball is to an outdoor game. But it still has its father-son charms: the high-low tinkles, making crosses with your streams. When all the pee doesn't land in the bowl (it won't), it will *definitely* be your job to clean it up.

252. Teach your child to endure name calling.

Your heart sinks when, at the playground, another child ridicules your kid (immediately, you flash to incidents from your own youth). But you know it's your job to help your child stand on his own two feet.

Instead of a wordy explanation of the ways of the world, try this: Say, "If you're an apple and someone says you're an orange, does that make you an orange?" Your kid will giggle and he'll struggle with the concept. But it's one worth learning, and eventually he'll get it.

253. Understand the Barney Curve.

As addictions go, your baby's Barney watching is relatively benign: easier on the teeth than bubble gum, easier on the lungs than cigarettes, but as tough on Mom and Pop as when you drove your parents crazy listening to the Doors full blast while staring at black-light posters. What undoes most parents is the severity of the craving and the glassy-eyed, drop-jawed, numbed expression on your kid's face while she's watching.

I say, relax. Indulge your kid by taking her to see Barney (live!) at the apex of her Barney obsession. I'll never forget bringing our three-year-old daughter and our two-month-old son to Radio City Music Hall. Amidst the swirling lights and swaying masses of youth, our daughter looked like a teenager at a Beatles concert. But her baby brother thought the whole thing loud and idiotic (okay, we were projecting), and my wife and I alternated pacing him in the lobby, where vendors were shamelessly hawking Barney regalia to pleading kids ("Buy it and I'll shut up, Daddy!") and depleted parents ("Be quiet or I won't buy anything!")

The addiction won't last forever. One day, your child will wake up and look at Barney with the incomprehension of a Buddhist monk standing on the floor of the stock exchange. "Yuck! It's Barney! Turn it off!" our daughter yelled at the TV. But alas, her infant brother was then in the throes of his own Barney addiction—and they had to slug it out until they were both cured the old-fashioned way: by age and time.

254. Fulfill your child's dream.

Most of the time, you'll have to be steady and reliable Dad, even to the point of being dull. And there'll be times you'll be Dad the jerk, and then there are times you'll get to be a hero.

My little kids were nearly inconsolable when our landlord wouldn't allow us to have a dog. (They'd already picked one out and named it—Peaches.) My wife put her arm over my shoulder. "You tried," she said. But for a father, not being able to fulfill a dream for his children is, well, a tough one to swallow.

Once in a while, if you want to really give your kids something to remember later on, let yourself be over-the-top. On this occasion, I had a grandiose inspiration. I dashed toward my kids' room and announced I would hire an animal trainer for my daughter's birthday, just two weeks off. Almost immediately, the tears dried up. I felt instantly terrific.

Had I promised too much?

The big day came and the animal trainer I'd hired arrived in a van with about thirty exotic creatures housed in boxes, ranging in size from a hatbox to a cargo trunk. He asked, "How many flights of stairs?" "Four," I said. He pointed to the largest suitcase. "Hope you're feeling athletic. My albino python weighs forty-five pounds. And he's just eaten dinner."

As I charged up and down the stairs, puffing and sweating, I felt charged with triumph. When I'd set down a box in our living room, I'd say to my kids (and to my wife, the zookeeper), "Don't open it. It might be a crocodile." My kids clapped and rocked back and forth in glee.

The other kids arrived and the show began. Waves of shrill screams erupted when my daughter volunteered to let a tarantula crawl over her chest and into her hair. Or when the boa constrictor wrapped itself four times around her tiny body so its head was beside my daughter's, its tongue flicking near her nervous smile. Or when the little crocodile opened wide so the kids could see down its throat.

All too soon, the party was over. I stood there for a few moments amidst the animal crates and chocolate cake crumbs and half-full cups of apple juice, feeling a sensation that might be particular to fathers: a swelling of the chest, a pride that I'd first felt when I watched our newborn daughter asleep in the nursery. There are moments that only mothers know: pregnancy, labor, delivery, breast-feeding. But equally, there are moments specific to fatherhood, and this was one of them. If only for an afternoon, I'd created a little kingdom for my kids.

WHEN YOU SAY, "I WANT MY KID TO HAVE A BETTER LIFE," MEAN EMOTIONAL AND SPIRITUAL—NOT MATERIAL.

---

255. *Take your kid crabbing.*

Here's one of life's simplest pleasures. Go to a fish store and ask for some fish scraps they can't sell. (They'll give you, say, the shoulder of a salmon.) Now, buy a fishnet for your kid, one with a small wooden handle that he can use to scoop. Buy fishing line and a couple of big hooks.

Head for the local pier, a dock in a bay, a marina. Showtime: Drop the chumming bait into the water. Bait your kid's hook, use a sinker, and drop it in nearby. Wait a few moments, then pull up. Depending on how much bait is on his hook, there may be between one and five crabs. Reach down with the net just as they are near the water's surface. Hoist the crabs onto the dock and let them scurry about. Or put them in a pail filled with seawater or help your kid shoo them back in the water.

One night, my kid and I stood on a dock in a deluge in rain slickers and hats, baiting a hook, pulling up our line, netting the feisty creatures, and then watching them scramble off the dock and back into the rain-pocked ocean.

This is the kind of moment together you and your child may remember for a long, long time.

256. Share your kid's new interests.

Here's what you can look forward to: If you remain open, your child will surprise you—and you'll grow, too.

Maybe it had something to do with crabbing together. Somehow, my son became entranced by fishing. So I took him out in my kayak to the fringes of a little pond, and we sat and sat and sat while we fished. One day, his reel spun wildly; we both jerked to attention, totally shocked that we actually caught a fish. He sat in my lap, reeling his fish in; I sensed his total joy. Unfortunately, I was completely unprepared—without net or fish tote bag—and he wanted to bring the fish home to live in our bathtub. Just as we were about to yank the kayak to the dock, the fish bolted, and my son burst into tears.

Now, we're both better prepared.

This fishing business is (for whatever reason) real father stuff. My dad took me to a trout farm in Wisconsin, which was a bit like a father bringing a son to a brothel and saying, "Go ahead and see if you can get lucky." If we'd written "hook" on a piece of paper and held it near the water, a fish would have bitten. What I like about fishing with my son is the down time: It's about the two of us together in a boat, waiting to see what will happen, and discovering that we don't have to bring anything home to have had a good time.

257. Tell your wife when you're moved by fatherhood.

A few years ago, after a major holiday, we got home, ripped off our fancy clothes, and headed off to pick blueberries. We were the only people there, high on a hill, the sun setting, and after we'd picked more than we could eat, give away to friends, and freeze, our kids began kicking a soccer ball on a vast field. In the late-day sun, I turned to my wife; a breeze was blowing through her hair and she smiled at me. I threw my arm over her shoulder and we watched our kids dancing across the field in the yellow light after the white ball. Behind them, hills toppled over one another into the blue distance. Finally, I said, "If there is a heaven, I bet it looks pretty much like this."

It's moments like that that fuel your marriage through the rougher spots.

258. Just tell her that you love her.

"We'll be lying in bed," my friend Jennifer said, "and I'll say to Bjorn, 'Tell me—even if you don't mean it.' 'What?' he'll say. 'Tell me you love me.' 'Okay. I love you.' 'How much do you love me?' 'I love you a lot.' 'Tell me more.' 'What more do you want to know?' And on and on . . . "

Women want romance. One female friend said to her husband, "Don't get cynical on Valentine's Day and tell me, 'It's a holiday made for Hallmark cards.' That's just not what I want to hear! I want chocolates. I want a note. I want the works!"

Be sure to write a love note to your wife on your anniversary, the anniversary of the day you met, and any other romantic dates (say, the day you moved into your home—you get the picture). Even if it feels redundant, give her a card and maybe a little gift on these dates. Don't forget!

CREATE A SPECIAL HANDSHAKE WITH YOUR KID. Find a combination of slapping fives or soul handshakes or . . . whatever you devise with your kid. It's a physical way of bonding you two, feeling like you're a team. Then keep it a secret between you.

---

259. Buy your wife a ring.

I don't care if it's a fancy ring or not (to me, simpler is better), but it's time you show your recommitment to your wife. Your wife knows that all the rules have changed since you got married, and she wants to know you accept the conditions. When you accepted your vows, your upper lip may have been trembling (or not), but you certainly had no idea what "for better or worse" meant until you had a baby.

Be sure to write a note—which will mean even more to her than the ring.

260. The day will come when you look at your wife and say, "You know, it's not so hard anymore."

Those frenetic early parenting days seem a million years ago, your child seems happily adjusted, Barney is out of your life (well . . . almost), your wife's figure is back, and life is on track. So what do you do?

Maybe this: You both slowly but simultaneously decide it's time you create another baby. (You don't listen to the voice in your head: *But you'll be working until you're seventy-five!*) Then, when you and your wife are entirely sure, you sweep her off her feet and carry her to bed. Her eyes will be glimmering and neither of you will believe what you're about to try to do . . . but that's perfectly right, too.

No coldly rational person would embark on this journey again, but who said you were rational? Sure, there'll be diapers and spats and sleep deprivation and times you'll want to rip the steering wheel off your car and eat it. The thing is, you two now know it's all worth it. Ease of life is fine and good—but it's not everything.

So with your child asleep in another room, you make love to your wife once again with no protection and you feel part of something special. With determination, will, and lots of luck, you'll make it. Congratulations. You're about to start over again.

ACKNOWLEDGMENTS

Special thanks to the following people for their invaluable contributions: Henry Ferris, my editor; Elizabeth Kaplan, my agent; and everyone at William Morrow, especially Michael Murphy, Sharyn Rosenblum, Ann Triestman, Lizz Pawlson, Marly Rusoff, and Rich Aquan.

I am grateful to friends and family who offered support, guidance, critical readings, and/or interviews: Liz Mutter, Gayle and Peter Grabell, Patty White, Arthur Montgomery, Valerie Cordy, Libby and Frampton Simons, Elin McCoy, Cynthia Krause, Miriam Cohen, and Susan Falk. Warm thanks to John Frederick Walker for his careful readings. Sincere gratitude to Jeff Moores for his illustrations and Greg Villepique for his copyediting. Collective thanks to all my friends for sharing their tales of early parenthood.

As always, thanks to my parents—for everything.

But the biggest thanks go to my wife and kids. To Jeannette, for being even more mysterious and beautiful in motherhood than before; to Isabelle, for totally erasing the misguided phrase "Terrible Twos" from our vocabulary; and to Benjamin, for never laughing when I got my fishing hook caught everywhere but in a fish's mouth.